Note: This **UNCLASSIFIED** handbook is designed to provide SERE students with information to review during the basic SERE course and as an aid for retention. SERE graduates are encouraged to periodical review this information and continue your SERE education from the recommended reading list

TABLE OF CONTENTS

QUICK REFERENCE CHECKLIST

DECIDE TO SURVIVE!

S – Size up the situation.
Physical condition
Adequate water intake
Injuries, Illness
Food
Surroundings
Equipment
U – Use all your senses, slow down and think.
R – Remember where you are.
V – Vanquish fear and panic.
I – Improvise and improve.
V – Value living.
A – Act like the natives.
L – Live by your training and experience

1. **IMMEDIATE ACTIONS**
   a. Assess immediate situation…**THINK BEFORE YOU ACT!**
   b. Take action to protect yourself from **Nuclear, Biological or Chemical** hazards. (See Chapter XI)
   c. Seek concealment.
   d. Assess medical condition; treat as necessary. (See Chapter X)
   e. Sanitize uniform of potentially compromising information.
   f. Sanitize area, hide equipment you are leaving.
   g. Apply camouflage.
   h. Move away from initial site; zigzag pattern recommended.
   i. Use terrain to advantage; communication and concealment.
   j. Find hold-up site.

2. **HOLD-UP SITE (See ChapterIX)**
   a. Reassess, treat injuries, inventory equipment.
   b. Review plan of action; establish priorities (See Chapter VI)
   c. Determine your current location.
   d. Improve camouflage.
   e. Focus thoughts on task(s) at hand.
   f. Execute plan of action…**STAY FLEXIBLE!**

1

3. CONCEALMENT (See Chapter IX)
    a. Select a place of cover and concealment providing:
        (1) Adequate cover; ground and air.
        (2) Safe distance from enemy positions and lines of communication.(LOCs)
        (3) Listening and observation point.
        (4) Multiple avenues of escape.
        (5) Protection from the environment.
        (6) Possible communication/signaling opportunities.
    b. Stay alert, maintain security.
    c. Drink water.

4. MOVEMENT (See Chapter IX)
    a. Travel slowly and deliberately.
    b. Do not leave evidence of travel, use noise and light discipline.
    c. Stay away from LOC's.
    d. Stop, Look, Listen, and Smell; take appropriate action.
    e. Move from one concealed area to another.
    f. Use evasion movement techniques (See Chapter ???)

5. COMMUNICATION AND SIGNALING (See Chapter VII)
    a. Communicate per theater communication procedures, particularly when considering transmitting in the "blind".
    b. Be prepared to use devices on short notice.
    c. Communication/signaling devices may compromise position.

6. RECOVERY OPERATIONS (See Chapter VI)
    a. Select site(s) IAW criteria in theater recovery plans.
    b. Ensure site is free of hazards; secure personal gear.
    c. Select best area for communications and signaling devices.
    d. Observe site for proximity to enemy activity and LOCs.
    e. Follow recovery force instructions.

CHAPTER I
CODE OF CONDUCT

The Code of Conduct represents a formal expression of the standards of military conduct understood and accepted by most countries for centuries. It serves as a guideline to be followed by all members of the armed forces, particularly when in a captured or detained status. It is professional and inspirational rather than a penal code. Failure to live up to the full extent of its obligations is not a criminal offense. Adequate authority exists under the Uniform Code of Military Justice for that malfeasance's which can be properly termed criminal acts. Should a service member engage in actions punishable under the UCMJ, they may be prosecuted under that statute, but not under the Code of Conduct. It is recognized that inhuman treatment and the application of psychological techniques have succeeded in individual cases in forcing involuntary departures from the standards set forth by the Code and can be expected to do so in the future. Notwithstanding these past and possible future departures, it would be unwise to officially advocate voluntary departures for any reason. The individual must be expected to adhere to both the spirit and the intent of the Code of Conduct to the full extent of their physical, mental, and moral resources. The wisdom of the Code of Conduct has been confirmed by former captives who found it a source of strength in situations of severe duress.

ARTICLE I

> **I am an American, fighting in the forces which guard my country and our way of life. I am prepared to give my life in their defense.**

Article I of the Code of Conduct apply to all service members at all times. A member of the armed forces has a duty to support the interests and oppose the enemies of the United States regardless of the circumstances, whether in active participation in combat or captivity.
Past experience of captured Americans reveal that honorable survival of captivity requires that a member possess a high degree of dedication and motivation. Maintaining these qualities requires knowledge of and a strong belief in its institutions and concepts. Possessing the dedication and motivation fostered by such beliefs and trust will enable prisoners to survive long, stressful periods of captivity and return to country and family honorably and with their self-esteem intact.

ARTICLE II

> **I will never surrender of my on free will. If in command I will never surrender the members of my command while they still have the means to resist.**

Members of the Armed Forces may never voluntarily surrender. Even when isolated and no longer able to inflict casualties on the enemy or otherwise defend themselves, it is their duty to evade capture and rejoin the nearest friendly force. When cut off, shot down or otherwise isolated in enemy controlled territory, they must make every effort to avoid capture. The courses of action available include concealment until recovered by friendly rescue forces, evasive travel to a friendly or neutral territory, and evasive travel to other pre-briefed areas.

The responsibility and authority of a commander never exceeds to the surrender of command, even if isolated, cut off or surrounded, while the unit still has the power to resist, break out, or evade to join friendly forces. Only when evasion by members is impossible and further fighting would lead only to their death with no significant loss to the enemy, might the means to resist or evade be considered exhausted.

Capture does not constitute a dishonorable act if all reasonable means of avoiding it have been exhausted and the only alternative is certain death.

ARTICLE III

If I am captured, I will continue to resist by all means available. I will make every effort to escape and aid others to escape. I will accept neither parole nor special favors from the enemy.

The duty of a member of the Armed Forces to continue resistance to enemy exploitation by all means available is not lessened by the misfortune of capture. Contrary to the 1949 Geneva Conventions, enemies which U.S. forces have engaged since 1949 have regarded the PW compound as an extension of the battlefield. The Prisoner of War (PW) must be prepared for this fact.

In disregarding provisions of the Geneva Conventions, the enemy has used a variety of tactics to exploit PW's for propaganda purposes or to obtain military information. Resistance to captor exploitation efforts is required by the Code of Conduct. Physical and mental harassment, general mistreatment and torture, medical neglect and political indoctrination have all been used against PW's in the past.

Under the guidance and supervision of the senior military person and PW organization, PWs must be prepared to take advantage of escape opportunities whenever they arise. In communal detention, the welfare of the PWs who will remain behind must be considered. A PW must "think escape," must try to escape if able to do so and must assist others to escape. The enemy has tried to tempt PWs to accept special favors or privileges not given to other PWs in return for statements or information desired by the enemy or for a pledge by the PW not to try to escape. A PW must not seek special privileges or accept special favors at the expense of his fellow PWs. Parole agreements and promises given the captor by a prisoner of war to fulfill stated conditions, such as not to bear arms or not to escape, in consideration of special privileges, such as release from captivity or lessened restraint. The United States does not authorize any service member to sign or enter into any such parole agreement

ARTICLE IV

If I become a prisoner of war, I will keep faith with my fellow prisoners. I will give no information or take or take part in any action which might be harmful to my comrades. If I am senior, I will take command. If not, I will obey the lawful orders of those appointed over me and will back them up in every way.

Officers and non-commissioned officers will continue to carry out their responsibilities and to exercise their authority in captivity. Informing or any other action detrimental to a fellow PW, is despicable and is expressly forbidden. Prisoners of war must especially avoid helping the enemy to identify fellow PWs who may have knowledge of value to the enemy and who may therefore, be made to suffer coercive interrogation.

Wherever located, PWs, for their own benefit, should organize in a military manner under the senior person eligible for command. The senior person (whether officer or enlisted) within the PW camp or with a group of PWs, shall assume command accordingly to rank without regard to military service. This responsibility and accountability may not be evaded.

When taking command, the senior person will inform the other PWs and will designate the chain of command. If the senior person is incapacitated or is otherwise unable to act for any reason, the next senior person will assume command. Every effort will be made to inform all PWs in the camp (or group) of the members of the chain of command who will represent them in dealing with enemy authorities. The responsibility of subordinates to obey the lawful orders of ranking American military personnel remains unchanged in captivity. The senior military person is required to represent the prisoners under his control in matters of camp administration, health, welfare and grievances. However, it must be borne constantly in mind that the enemy has often viewed PWs as valuable sources of military information and of propaganda that can be used to further the enemy's war effort.

ARTICLE V

> **When questioned, should I become a prisoner of war, I am required to give name, rank, service number and date of birth. I will evade answering further questions to the utmost of my ability. I will make no oral or written statements disloyal to my country and its allies or harmful to their cause.**

When questioned, a prisoner of war is required by the Geneva Conventions, this Code and is permitted by the UCMJ to give name, rank, service number and date of birth. Under the Geneva Conventions, the enemy has no right to try to force a PW to provide any additional information. However, it is unrealistic to expect a PW to remain confined for years reciting only name, rank, service number and date of birth. There are many PW camp situations in which certain types of conversation with the enemy are permitted. For example, a PW is allowed, but not required by this Code, the UCMJ or the Geneva Conventions, to fill out a Geneva Conventions capture card, to write letters home and to communicate with captors on matters of health and welfare.

Accordingly, each prisoner must exercise great caution when filling out a capture card, when conducting authorized communication with the captor and when writing letters. A PW must resist, avoid or evade, even when physically and mentally coerced, all enemy efforts to secure statements or actions that will further the enemy's cause.

A PW should recognize that any confession signed or any statement made may be used by the enemy as part of a false accusation that the captive is a war criminal rather than a PW. Moreover, certain countries have made reservations to the Geneva Conventions, in which they assert that a war criminal conviction has the effect of depriving the convicted individual of prisoner of war status, thus removing them from protection under the Geneva Conventions. They thus revoke the right to repatriation until a prison sentence is served.

Such statements or actions constitute giving the enemy unauthorized information. Examples of statements or actions PWs should resist include oral or written confessions, questionnaires, personal history statements, propaganda recordings and broadcast appeals to other prisoners of war to comply with improper demands, appeals for surrender or parole, self-criticisms, oral or written statements, communication on behalf of the enemy or harmful to the United States, it's allies, the Armed Forces or other PW's.

Experience has shown that even when coerced beyond name, rank, service number, date of birth and claims of inabilities, it is possible to thwart an interrogator's efforts to obtain useful information by the use of certain additional ruses and stratagems, provided there is a will to resist.

If a PW finds that, under intense coercion, unauthorized information was unwillingly or accidentally disclosed, then the member should attempt to recover and resist with a fresh line of mental defense.

ARTICLE VI

I will never forget that I am an American, fighting for freedom, responsible for my actions and dedicated to the principles which make my country free. I will trust in my God and in the United States of America.

A member of the Armed Forces remains responsible for personal actions at all times. This Article is designed to assist members of the Armed Forces to fulfill their responsibilities and to survive captivity with honor. The Code of Conduct does not conflict with the UCMJ and the latter continues to apply to each military service member during captivity (or in other hostile detention). A member of the Armed Forces who is captured has a continuing obligation to resist all attempts to indoctrination and to remain loyal to country, service and unit. Every member of the Armed Forces of the United States should understand that members can be held legally accountable for personal actions while detained.

Upon repatriation, PW's can expect their actions to be subject to review, both as to circumstances of capture and as to conduct during detention. The purpose of each interview is to recognize misconduct. The reviews will be conducted with due regard for the rights of the individual and consideration for the conditions of captivity.

Every member of the Armed Forces of the United States should understand the importance of ensuring that their personal affairs and family matters (pay, powers of attorney, will, car payments and children's schooling) are kept current through discussion, counseling or filing of documents prior to being exposed to risk of capture. That failure to accomplish these has resulted in an almost overwhelming sense of guilt on the part of the PWs, and has placed unnecessary hardship on family members.

The national policy expressed by the President of the United States in promulgating the Code of Conduct:

"No American prisoner of war will be forgotten by the United States. Every available means will be employed by our government to establish contact with, to support and to obtain the release of all our prisoners of war. Furthermore, the laws of the United States provide for the support and care of dependents of the Armed Forces including those who become prisoners of war. I assure dependents of such prisoners that these laws will continue to provide their welfare."

6

CHAPTER II
GENEVA CONVENTIONS
RELATIVE TO THE TREATMENT
OF PRISONERS OF WAR
1949

EXTRACT OF PERTINENT ARTICLES

NOTE: The complete Article is quoted, unless otherwise stated.

LEGAL STATUS

ARTICLE 1. The High Contracting Parties undertake to respect and to ensure respect for the present Convention in all circumstances.

STUDENT NOTE: Your knowledge of these Articles is what makes the Geneva Conventions work. Your persistence in demanding your rights under these Articles coupled with the very powerful influence of world opinion could very well force captors who are signatories, and not adhering to Article 1, to comply. If your persistence fails, the information gathered upon repatriation, could be damaging to that country in the form of legal sanctions. Any one of you could be duty bound by the Code of Conduct to represent others in obtaining the legal rights listed herein.

ARTICLE 2 In addition to the provisions which shall be implemented in peacetime, the present Convention shall apply to all cases of declared war or of any other armed conflict which may arise between two or more of the High Contracting Parties, even if the state of war is not recognized by one of them.

The Convention shall also apply to all cases of partial or total occupation of the territory of the High Contracting Party, even if the said occupation meets with no armed resistance.

Although one of the Powers in conflict may not be a party to the present Convention, the Powers who are parties thereto shall remain bound by it in their mutual relations. They shall futhermore be bound by the Convention in relation to the said Power, if the latter accepts and applies the provisions thereof.

ARTICLE 4.

A. Prisoners of war, in the sense of the present Convention, are persons belonging to one of the following categories, who have fallen into the power of the enemy:

(1) Members of the armed forces of a Party to the conflict, as well as members of militias or volunteer corps forming part of such armed forces.

(2) Members of other militias and members of other volunteer corps, including those of organized resistance movements, belonging to a Party to the conflict and operating in or outside their own territory, even if this territory is occupied, provided that such militias or volunteer corps, including such organized resistance movements, fulfills the following conditions:

(a) that of being commanded by a person responsible for his subordinates;

(b) that of having a fixed distinctive sign recognizable at a distance;

(c) that of carrying arms openly;

(d) that of conducting their operations in accordance with the laws and customs of war.

(3) Members of regular armed forces who profess allegiance to a government or an authority not recognized by the Detaining Power.

(4) Persons who accompany the armed forces without actually being members thereof, such as civilian members of military aircraft crews, war correspondents, supply contractors, members of labor units or of services responsible for the welfare of the armed forces, provided that they have received authorization from the armed forces which they accompany, who shall provide them for that purpose with an identity card similar to the annexed model.

(5) Members of crews, including masters, pilots and apprentices, of the merchant marine and the crews of civil aircraft of the Parties to the conflict, who do not benefit by more favorable treatment under any other provisions of international law.

(6) Inhabitants of a non-occupied territory, who on the approach of the enemy spontaneously take up arms to resist the invading forces, without having had time to form themselves into regular armed units provided they carry arms openly and respect the laws and customs of war.

B. The following shall likewise be treated as prisoners of war under the present convention:

(1) Persons belonging, or having belonged to the armed forces of the occupied country, if the occupying Power considers it necessary by reason of such allegiance to intern them, even though it has originally liberated them while hostilities were going on outside the territory it occupies, in particular where such persons have made an unsuccessful attempt to rejoin the armed forces to which they belong and which are engaged in combat, or where they fail to comply with a summons made to them with a view to internment.

(2) The persons belonging to one of the categories enumerated in the present Article, who have been received by neutral or non-belligerent Powers on their territory and whom these Powers are required to intern international law, without prejudice to any more favorable treatment which these Powers may choose to give and with the exception of Articles 8, 10, 15, 30, fifth paragraph 58-67, 92, 126 and, where diplomatic relations exist between the Parties to the conflict and the neutral or non-belligerent Power concerned, those Articles concerning the Protecting Power. Where such diplomatic relations exist, the Parties to a conflict on whom these persons depend shall be allowed to perform towards them the functions of a Protecting Power as provided in the present Convention, without prejudice to the functions which these Parties normally exercise in conformity with diplomatic and consular usage and treaties.

C. This Article shall in no way affect the status of medical personnel and chaplains as provided for in Article 33 of the present Convention.

ARTICLE 7. Prisoners of war may under no circumstances renounce in part or in entirety the rights secured to them by the present Convention and by the special agreements referred to in the foregoing Article, if such there were.

ARTICLE 12. Prisoners of war are in the hands of the enemy Power, but not of the individuals or military units who have captured them. Irrespective of the individual responsibilities that may exist, the Detaining Power is responsible for the treatment given them. Prisoners of war may only be transferred by the Detaining Power to a Power which is a party to the Convention and after the Detaining Power has satisfied itself of the willingness and ability of such transferee Power to apply the Convention. When prisoners of war are transferred under such circumstances, responsibility for the application of the Convention rests on the Power accepting them while they are in its custody. Nevertheless, if that Power fails to carry out the provisions of the Convention in any important respect, the Power by whom the prisoners of war were transferred shall, upon being notified by the Protecting Power, take effective measures to correct the situation or shall request the return of the prisoners of war. Such requests must be complied with.

ARTICLE 13. Prisoners of war must at all times be humanely treated. Any unlawful act or omission by the Detaining Power causing death or seriously endangering the health of a prisoner in its custody is prohibited and will be regarded as a serious breach of the present Convention. In particular, no prisoner may be subjected to physical mutilation or to medical or scientific experiments of any kind which are not justified by the medical, dental or hospital treatment of the prisoner concerned and carried out in his interest. Likewise, prisoners of war must at all times be protected, particularly against acts of violence or intimidation and against insults and public curiosity. Measures of reprisal against prisoners of war are prohibited.

INTERROGATION

ARTICLE 17. Every prisoner of war, when questioned on the subject, is bound to give only his surname, first name and rank, date of birth and army, regimental, personal or serial number or failing this, equivalent information. If he willfully infringes this rule, he may render himself liable to a restriction of privileges accorded to his rank or status. Each Party to a conflict is required to furnish the persons under its jurisdiction who are liable to become prisoners of war with an identity card showing the owner's surname, first names, rank, army, regimental, personal or serial number or equivalent information and date of birth. The identity card may bear as well, any other information the party to the conflict may wish to add concerning persons belonging to its armed forces. As far as possible the card shall measure 6.5 x 10 cm. and shall be issued in duplicate. The identity card shall be shown by the prisoner of war upon demand, but may in no case be taken from him. No physical or mental torture, nor any other form of coercion, may be inflicted on prisoners of war to secure from them information of any kind whatever. Prisoners of war who refuse to answer may not be threatened, insulted or exposed to unpleasant or disadvantageous treatment of any kind to prisoners of war who, owing to their physical or mental condition, are unable to state their identity, shall be handed over to the medical service. The identity of such prisoners shall be established by all possible means, subject to the provisions of the preceding paragraph. The questioning of prisoners of war shall be carried out in a language which they understand.

ARTICLE 25 (Extract). Prisoners of war shall be quartered under conditions as favorable as those for the forces of the Detaining Power who are billeted in the same area. The said conditions shall make allowance for the habits and customs of the prisoners and shall in no case be prejudicial to their health. The foregoing provisions shall apply in particular to the dormitories of prisoners of war in regards to both total surface and minimum cubic space and the general installations, bedding and blankets. The premises provided for the use of prisoners of war individually or collectively, shall be entirely protected from dampness and adequately heated and lighted, in particular, between dusk and lights out. All precautions must be taken against danger of fire.

FOOD

ARTICLE 26. The basic daily rations shall be sufficient in quantity, quality and variety to keep prisoners of war in good health and to prevent loss of weight or the development of nutritional deficiencies. Account shall also be taken of the habitual diet of the prisoners. The Detaining Power shall supply prisoners of war who work with such additional rations as may be necessary for the labor on which they are employed. Sufficient drinking water shall be supplied to prisoners of war. The use of tobacco shall be permitted. Prisoners of war shall, so far as possible, be associated with the preparation of their meals; they may be employed for that purpose in the kitchens. Furthermore, they shall be given the means of preparing, themselves, the additional food in their possession. Adequate premises shall be provided for messing. Collective disciplinary measures affecting food are prohibited.

CLOTHING

ARTICLE 27 (Extract). Clothing, underwear and footwear shall be supplied to prisoners of war in sufficient quantities by the Detaining Power, which shall make allowance for the climate of the region where prisoners are detained.

MEDICAL

ARTICLE 29. The Detaining Power shall be bound to take all sanitary measures necessary to ensure the cleanliness and healthfulness of camps and to prevent epidemics. Prisoners of war shall have for their use, day and night, conveniences, which conform to the rules of hygiene and are maintained in a constant state of cleanliness. In any camps in which women prisoners of war are accommodated, separate conveniences shall be provided for them. Also, apart from the baths and showers with which the camps shall be furnished, prisoners of war shall be provided with sufficient water and soap for their personal toilet and for washing their personal laundry; the necessary installations, facilities and time shall be granted them for that purpose.

ARTICLE 30. Every camp shall have an adequate infirmary where prisoners of war may have the attention they require, as well as appropriate diet. Isolation wards shall, if necessary, be set aside for cases of contagious or mental disease. Prisoners of war suffering from serious disease or whose condition necessitates special treatment, a surgical operation or hospital care, must be admitted to any military or civilian medical unit where such treatment can be given, even if their repatriation is contemplated in the near future. Special facilities shall be afforded for the care to be given to the disabled, in particular to the blind and for their rehabilitation, pending repatriation. Prisoners of war shall have the attention, preferably of medical personnel of the Power on which they depend and, if possible, of their nationality. Prisoners of war may not be prevented from presenting themselves to medical authorities for examination.

ARTICLE 31. Medical inspections of prisoners of war shall be held at least once a month. They shall include the checking and the recording of the weight of each prisoner of war. Their purpose shall be, in particular, to supervise the general state of health, nutrition and cleanliness of prisoners and to detect contagious diseases, especially tuberculosis, malaria and venereal disease. For this purpose the most efficient methods available shall be employed, e.g., periodic mass miniature radiography for the early detection of tuberculosis.

ARTICLE 32. Prisoners of war who, though not attached to the medical service of their armed forces, are physicians, surgeons, dentists, nurses or medical orderlies, may be required by the Detaining Power to exercise their medical function in the interests of prisoners of war dependent of the same Power. In that case they shall continue to be prisoners of war, but shall receive the same treatment as corresponding medicinal personnel retained by the Detaining Power. They shall be exempted from any other work under Article 49.

RELIGION

ARTICLE 33. Members of the medical personnel and chaplains while retained by the detaining power with a view to assisting prisoners of war shall not be considered prisoners of war. They shall, however, receive as a minimum the benefits and protection of the present convention.

ARTICLE 34. Prisoners of war shall enjoy complete latitude in the exercise of their religious duties, including attendance at the service of their faith, on condition that they comply with the disciplinary routine prescribed by the military authorities. Adequate premises shall be provided where religious services may be held.

EDUCATION

ARTICLE 38. While respecting the individual preferences of every prisoner, the Detaining Power shall encourage the practice of intellectual, educational and recreational pursuits, sports and games amongst prisoners and shall take the measures necessary to ensure the exercise thereof by providing them with adequate premises and necessary equipment.

MILITARY COURTESY

ARTICLE 39. Every prisoner of war shall be put under the immediate authority of a responsible commissioned officer belonging to the regular armed forces of the Detaining Power. Such officer shall have in his possession a copy of the present Convention; he shall ensure that its provisions are known to the camp staff and the guards shall be responsible, under the direction of his government, for its application. Prisoners of war, with the exception of officers, must salute and show to all officers of the Detaining Power the external marks of respect provided for by the regulations applying to their own forces officer prisoners of war are bound to salute only officers of a higher rank of the Detaining Power; they must, however, salute the camp commander regardless of his rank.

ARTICLE 40. The wearing of badges of rank and nationality, as well as of decorations, shall be permitted.

ARTICLES POSTED

ARTICLE 41. In every camp, the text of the present Convention and its Annexes and the contents of any special agreement provided for in Article 6 shall be posted, in the prisoners' own language, in places where all may read them. Copies shall be supplied, on request, to the prisoners who cannot have access to the copy which has been posted. Regulations, orders, notices and publications of every kind relating to the conduct of prisoners of war shall be issued to them in a language which they understand. Such regulations, orders and publications shall be posted in the manner described above and copies shall be handed to the prisoners' representative. Every order and command addressed to prisoners of war individually must likewise be given in a language which they understand.

LABOR

ARTICLE 49. The Detaining Power may utilize the labor of prisoners of war who are physically fit, taking into account their age, sex, rank and physical aptitude and with a view particularly to maintaining them in a good state of physical and mental health. Noncommissioned officers who are prisoners of war shall only be required to do supervisory work. Those not so required may ask for other suitable work which shall, so far as possible, be found for them. If officers or persons of equivalent status ask for suitable work, it shall be found for them, so far as possible, but they may under no circumstances be compelled to work.

ARTICLE 50. Besides work connected with camp administration, installation or maintenance, prisoners of war may be compelled to do only, such work as is included in the following classes:

(a) agriculture;

(b) industries connected with the production or the extraction of raw material and manufacturing industries, with the exception of metallurgical, machinery and chemical industries; public works and building operations which have no military character or purpose;

(c) transport and handling of stores which are not military in character or purpose;

(d)commercial business, and arts and crafts;

(e)domestic service;

(f)public utility services having no military character or purpose.

Should the above provisions be infringed, prisoners of war shall be allowed to exercise their right of complaint, in conformity with Article 78.

DANGEROUS WORK

ARTICLE 52. Unless he be a volunteer, no prisoner of war may be employed on labor which is of an unhealthy or dangerous nature. No prisoners of war shall be assigned to labor, which would be looked upon as humiliating for a member of the Detaining Power's own forces.

The removal of mines or similar devices shall be considered as dangerous labor.

CAPTURE CARDS

ARTICLE 70. Immediately upon capture, or not more than one week after arrival at a camp, even if it is a transit camp, likewise in case of sickness or transfer to hospital or to another camp, every prisoners of war shall be enabled to write direct to his family, on the one hand and to the Central Prisoners of War Agency provided for in Article 123, on the other hand, a card similar, if possible, to the model annexed to the present Convention, informing his relatives of his capture, address and state of health. The said cards shall be forwarded as rapidly as possible and may not be delayed in any manner.

MAIL

ARTICLE 71 (Extract). Prisoners of war shall be allowed to send and receive letters and cards. If the Detaining Power deems it necessary to limit the number of letters and cards sent by each prisoner of war, the said number shall not be less than two letters and four cards monthly, exclusive of capture cards provided for in Article 70 and conforming as closely as possible to the models annexed to the present Convention. Further limitations may be imposed only if the Protecting Power is satisfied that it would be in the interests of the prisoners of war concerned to do so owing to difficulties of translation caused by the Detaining Power's inability to find sufficient qualified linguists to carry out the necessary censorship. If limitations must be placed on the correspondence addressed to prisoners of war, they may be ordered only by the Power on which the prisoner depends, possibly at the request of the Detaining Power. Such letters and cards must be conveyed by the most rapid method at the disposal of the Detaining Power; they may not be delayed or retained for disciplinary reasons.

PACKAGES

ARTICLE 72 (Extract). Prisoners of war shall be allowed to receive by post or by any other means individual parcels or collective shipments containing, in particular, food-stuffs, clothing, medical supplies and articles of religious, educational or recreational character which may meet their needs, including books, devotional articles, scientific equipment, examination papers, musical instruments, sports outfits and material allowing prisoners of war to pursue their studies or their cultural activities.

ARTICLE 76. The censoring of correspondence addressed to prisoners of war or dispatched by them shall be done as quickly as possible. Mail shall be censored only by the dispatching State and the receiving State, and once only by each. The examination of consignments intended for prisoners of war shall not be carried out under conditions that will expose the goods printed or matter, it shall be done in the presence of the addressee, or of a fellow-prisoner duly delegated by him. The delivery to prisoners of individual or collective consignments shall not be delayed under the pretext of difficulties of censorship, Any prohibition of correspondence ordered by Parties to the conflict, either for military or political reason, shall be only temporary and its duration shall be as short as possible.

PRISONER REPRESENTATIVES

ARTICLE 78. Prisoners of war shall have the right to make known to the military authorities in whose power they are, their requests regarding the conditions of captivity to which they are subjected. They shall also have the unrestricted right to apply to the representatives of the Protecting Powers either through their prisoners representative or, if they consider it necessary, direct, in order to draw their attention to any points on which they may have complaints to make regarding their conditions of captivity. These requests and complaints shall not be limited nor considered to be a part of the correspondence quota referred to in Article 71. They must be transmitted immediately. Even if they are recognized to be unfounded, they may not give rise to any punishment.
Prisoners' representatives may send periodic reports on the situation in the camps and the needs of the prisoners of war to the representatives of the Protecting Powers.

ARTICLE 79. In all places where there are prisoners of war, except in those where there are officers the prisoners shall freely elect by secret ballot, every six months and also in cases of vacancies, prisoners represented entrusted with representing them before the military authorities, the protecting powers the international committee of the red cross and any other organization which may assist them. The prisoner's representative shall be eligible for reelection. (**NOTE**: this conflicts with the Article IV of Code of Conduct, which states the senior soldier will take charge)
In camps for officers and persons of equivalent status or in mixed camps, the senior officer among the prisoners of war shall be recognized as the camp prisoner representative. In camps for officers one shall

14

assist him or more advisors chosen by the officers; in mixed camps, his assistants shall be chosen from among those prisoners of war who are not officers. Every representative must be approved by the detaining power before he has the right to commence his duties. Where the detaining power refuses to approve a prisoner of war elected by his fellow prisoners of war, it must inform the protecting power of the reason for refusal. In all cases the prisoner representative must have the same nationality, and language and customs as the prisoners of war for which he represents. Thus prisoners of war distributed in different sections of the camp according to their nationality language and customs shall have for their section their own prisoner representative, in accordance with the fore going paragraphs.

ARTICLE 81. Prisoners' representatives shall not be required to perform any other work, if the accomplishment of their duties is thereby made more difficult. Prisoners' representatives may appoint from amongst the prisoners such assistants as they may require. All material facilities shall be granted them, particularly a certain freedom of movement necessary for the accomplishment of their duties (inspection of labor detachments, receipt of supplies, etc.) Prisoner representatives shall be permitted to visit premises where prisoners of war are detained, and every prisoner of war shall have the right to consult freely his prisoners' representative. All facilities shall likewise be accorded to the prisoners' representatives for communication by post and telegraph with the detaining authorities, the Protecting Powers, the International Committee of the Red Cross and their delegates, the Mixed Medical Commissions and representatives of labor detachments shall enjoy the same facilities for communication with the prisoners' representatives of the principal camp. Such communications shall not be restricted, nor considered as forming a part of the quota mentioned in Article 71. Prisoners' representatives who are transferred shall be allowed a reasonable time to acquaint their successors with current affairs. In case of dismissal, the reasons therefore shall be communicated to the Protecting Power.

LAWS OF DETAINING POWER

ARTICLE 82. A prisoner of war shall be subject to the laws, regulations and orders in force in the armed forces of the Detaining Power; the Detaining Power shall be justified in taking judicial or disciplinary measures in respect of any offense committed by a prisoner of war against such laws, regulations or orders. However, no proceedings or punishments contrary to the provisions of this Chapter shall be allowed. If any law, regulation or order of the Detaining Power shall declare acts committed by a prisoner of war to be punishable, whereas the same acts would not be punishable if committed by a member of the forces of the Detaining Power, such acts shall entail disciplinary punishment only.

ARTICLE 85. Prisoners of war prosecuted under the laws of the Detaining Power for acts committed prior to capture shall retain, **EVEN IF CONVICTED**, the benefits of the present Convention.

NOTE: Certain nations have important reservations of this article. These countries insist any prisoner of war convicted of an **ALLEGED** war crime under the laws of the restraining power loses the protection afforded of the G C. This means **ANY** admission by a PW is subject to interpretation by a capturing power. If it suits the purpose, the country making the reservation can interpret the normal combat duties of a soldier as war crimes. Even if the charged PW is given a trial, the results and sentence are predetermined, as

THE ONLY EVIDENCE CONSIDERED IS THE PRISONER'S ADMISSION.

DISCIPLINARY SANCTIONS

ARTICLE 89. The disciplinary punishments applicable to prisoners of war are the following:

(1) A fine which shall not exceed 50 percent of the advances of pay and working pay which the prisoner of war would otherwise receive under the provisions of Article 60 and 62 during a period of not more than 30 days.

(2) Discontinuance of privileges granted over and above treatment provided for by the present Convention.

(3) Fatigue duties not exceeding two hours daily.

(4) Confinement The punishment referred to under (3) shall not be applied to officers.

In no case shall disciplinary punishments be inhuman, brutal or dangerous to the health of prisoners of war.

ARTICLE 90. The duration of any single (disciplinary) punishment shall in no case exceed 30 days. Any period of confinement awaiting the hearing of a disciplinary offense or the award of disciplinary punishment shall be deducted from an award pronounced against a prisoner of war. The maximum of 30 days provided above may not be exceeded, even if the prisoner of war is answerable for several acts at the same time when he is awarded punishment, whether such acts are related or not. The period between the pronouncing of an award of disciplinary punishment and its execution shall not exceed one month. When a prisoner of war is awarded a further disciplinary punishment, a period of at least three days shall elapse-between the execution of any two of the punishments, if the duration of one of these are ten days or more.

ESCAPE

ARTICLE 91. The escape of a prisoner of war shall be deemed to have succeeded when:

(1) He has joined the armed forces of the Power on which he depends or those of an ally of the said Power.

(2) He has left the territory under the control of the Detaining Power on which he depends or those of an ally of said Power.

(3)He has joined a ship flying the flag of the Power on which he depends or of an allied Power, in the territorial waters of the Detaining Power, the said ship not being under the control of the last named Power. Prisoners of war who have made attempts to escape in the sense of this Article and who are recaptured, shall not be liable to any punishment in respect of their previous escape.

ARTICLE 92. A prisoner of war who attempts to escape and is recaptured before having made good his escape in the sense of Article 91 shall be liable only to a disciplinary punishment in respect of this act, even if it is a repeated offense. A prisoner of war who is recaptured shall be handed over without delay to the competent military authority. Article 88, fourth paragraph, notwithstanding, prisoners of war punished as a result of an unsuccessful escape shall be subjected to special surveillance. Such surveillance shall not affect the state of their health, must be undergone in a prisoner of war camp and must not entail the suppression of any of the safeguards granted them by the present Convention.

NOTE: Offenses committed by PWs with the sole intention of facilitating their escape and which do not entail any violence against life or limb, such as offenses against public property, theft without intention of self-enrichment, the drawing up of false papers or the wearing of civilian clothing shall occasion disciplinary punishment only. The use of weapons against PWs, especially those attempting to escape, shall constitute an extreme by warnings. Killing during an escape can be punished by death.
If an escape is successful and the successful escapee is later recaptured, he may be subject to judicial action for those offenses entailing violence to life or limb or not otherwise within Article 93, GPW.
It should be noted that a soldier successfully effecting an escape is again a combatant (his legal status) and subject to the law of war. Killing of civilians or other breaches of the Conventions, to effect his escape subject him to prosecution under the Uniform Code of Military Justice. (Articles 42, 91, 93 GPW)

ARTICLE 93. Escape or attempt to escape, even if it is a repeated offense, shall not be deemed an aggravating circumstance if the prisoner of war is subjected to trial by judicial proceedings in respect of an offense committed during his escape or attempt to escape. In conformity with the principle stated in Article 83, offenses committed by prisoners of war with the sole intention of facilitating their escape and which do not entail any violence against life or limb, such as offenses against public property, theft without intention of self-enrichment, the drawing up of false papers or the wearing of civilian clothing, shall occasion disciplinary punishment only.

ARTICLE 97. Prisoners of war shall not in any case be transferred to penitentiary establishments (prisons, penitentiaries, convict prisons, etc.) to undergo disciplinary punishment therein. All premises in which disciplinary punishments are undergone shall conform to the sanitary requirements set forth in Article 25. A prisoner of war undergoing punishment shall be enabled to keep himself in a state of cleanliness, in conformity with Article 29. Officers and persons of equivalent status shall not be lodged in the same quarters as non- commissioned officers or men. Women prisoners of war undergoing disciplinary punishment shall be confined in separate quarters from male prisoners of war and shall be under the immediate supervision of women.

ARTICLE 126. Representatives or delegates of the Protecting Powers shall have permission to go to all places where prisoners of war may be, particularly to places of interment, imprisonment and labor, and shall have access to all premises occupied by prisoners of war; they shall also be allowed to go to the places of departure, passage and arrival of prisoners who are being transferred. They shall be able to interview the prisoners, and in particular the prisoners' representatives, without witnesses, either personally or through an interpreter. Representatives and delegates of the Protecting Powers shall have full liberty to select the places they wish to visit. The duration and frequency of these visits shall not be restricted. Visits may not be prohibited except for reasons of imperative military necessity, and then only as an exceptional and temporary measure. The Detaining Power and the Power on which the said prisoners of war depend may agree, if necessary, that compatriots of these prisoners of war be permitted to participate in the visits. The delegates of the International Committee of the Red Cross shall enjoy the same prerogatives. The appointment of such delegates shall be submitted to the approval of the Power detaining the prisoners of war to be visited.

TABLE OF UCMJ PUNITIVE ARTICLES
OF SPECIFIC APPLICABILITY TO
CODE OF CONDUCT TYPE SITUATIONS

ARTICLE NO.	DESCRIPTION
Article 85	Desertion by any member of the Armed Forces.
Article88	Use of contemptuous words by an officer against the President, Vice-President or other government official specifically identified.
Article 89	Disrespect by any member of the Armed Forces of his superior commissioned officer.
Article 90	Disobedience by any member of the Armed Forces of his superior commissioned officer.
Article 91	Insubordinate conduct by any warrant officer or enlisted member of the Armed Forces toward a warrant officer, non-commissioned officer or petty officer while that officer is in the execution of their office.
Article 92	(a) Failure of any member of the Armed Forces to obey a lawful General Order or other lawful order which does not qualify as a General Order. (b) Dereliction of duty by any member of the Armed Forces.
Article 94	Mutiny or sedition by any member of the Armed Forces.
Article 99	Misbehavior before the enemy by any member of the Armed Forces. (This article includes such acts of misbehavior as shamefully surrendering a command, casting away arms or ammunition and willful failure to do one's utmost to engage the enemy.)
Article 100	Compelling the surrender of command, without proper authority, by any member

of the Armed Forces. (This article includes communicating or holding any intercourse with the enemy without proper authority to do so.)

Article 104   Aiding the enemy by any member of the Armed Forces. (This article includes communicating or holding any intercourse with the enemy without proper authority to do so.)

Article 105   Misconduct by any member of the Armed Forces while held as a prisoner of war. (This article includes engaging in any act as a POW for the purpose of securing more favorable treatment from the enemy, if that act is also detrimental to fellow POW's.)

Article 133   The general article concerning conduct unbecoming an officer.

Article 134   The general article applicable to all members of the Armed Forces which concerns conduct prejudicial to the good order and discipline in the Armed Forces and conduct of a nature likely to bring discredit upon the Armed Forces of the United States.

Chapter III
Water

1. **Water Requirements**
   a. Drink as much water as possible (min 2 quarts per day) to maintain fluid level.
   b. Exertion, heat, injury or illnesses requires a greater need for water intake.

Note: Pale yellow urine indicates adequate hydration.

---

2. **Water Procurement**
   a. Water sources:
      (1) Surface water (streams, lakes and springs).
      (2) Precipitation (rain, snow, dew, sleet) (see FigureVII-1).

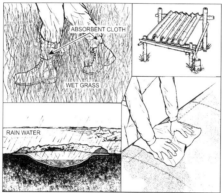

Figure VII-1. Water Procurement

      (3) Subsurface (wells and cisterns).
      (4) When no surface water is available, look for ground water (see Figure VII-2):

Figure VII-2. Water Indicators

20

(a) Abundance of lush green vegetation.

(b) Drainage's and low-lying areas.

(c) "V" intersecting game trails often point to water.

(d) Presence of swarming insects indicates water is near.

(e) Bird flight in the early morning or late afternoon might indicate the direction to water.

b. Obtaining water from snow or ice:

  (1) Do not eat ice or snow:

   (a) Lowers body temperature.

   (b) Induces dehydration.

   (c) Causes minor cold injury to lips and mouth.

  (2) Use a water generator (see Figure VII-3):

  (3) Melt ice or snow with body heat:

   (a) Use waterproof container.

   (b) Place between layers of clothing.

   (c) Do not place next to the skin.

  (4) Melting snow with fire:

   (a) Stir frequently to prevent damaging container.

   (b) Adding hot rocks or water speeds the process.

Figure VII-3. Water Generator

  (5) Sea ice (use old sea ice) (see Figure VII-4).

OLD SEA ICE	NEW SEA ICE
Bluish or blackish	Milky or grey
Shatters easily	Doesn't break easily
Rounded corners	Sharp edges
Tastes relatively salt-free	Tastes extremely salty

Figure VII-4

c. Open seas:
  (1) Precipitation:
    (a) Drink as much as possible.
    (b) Catch rain in spray shields and life raft covers.
    (c) Collect dew off raft.
  (2) Use issued sources.
  (3) Old sea ice or iceberg (See Figure VII-4).
  (4) Do not drink:
    (a) Urine.
    (b) Fish juices.
    (c) Blood.
    (d) Sea water.
    (e) Alcohol.
d. Tropical areas:
  (1) All open sources previously mentioned.
  (2) Vegetation:
    (a) Plants with hollow sections can collect moisture.
    (b) Leaning tree. Cloth absorbs rain running down tree and drips into container (see Figure VII-5).

Figure VII-5. Leaning Tree

    (c) Banana plants.
    (d) Water trees (avoid milky sap):
      • Tap before dark. Let sap stop running and harden during the daytime.
      • Produce most water at night.
      • For evasion situations, bore into the roots and collect water.
    (e) Vines (see Figure VII-6A):
      • Cut bark - do not use milky sap.
      • If juice is clear and water like, cut as large a piece of vine as possible, cutting the top first.
      • Pour into hand to check smell, color, and taste to determine if drinkable.
      • Do not touch vine to lips.
      • When water flow stops, cut off 6 inches of opposite end, water will flow again.

(f) Old bamboo:
- Shake and listen for water.
- Bore hole at bottom of section to obtain the water.
- Cut out entire section to carry with you.
- Filter and purify.

(g) Green bamboo (see Figure VII-6B).

Figure VII-6 A & B. Water Vines and Green Bamboo

(h) Along the coast, obtain water by:
- Digging a beach well (see Figure VII-7).
- Liquid contained in green coconuts (ripe coconuts may cause diarrhea).

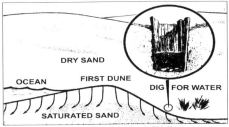

Figure VII-7. Beach Well

e. Dry areas:
(1) Solar still (see Figure VII-8).
(2) Foliage bag (see Figure VII-9).

Note: Do not use poisonous/toxic plants in any still or bag

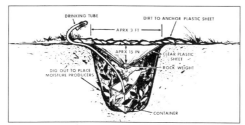

Figure VII-8. Solar Still

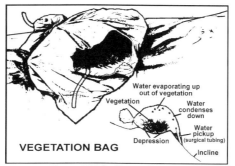

Figure VII-9. Vegetation Bag

(3) Transpiration bag (see Figure VII-10):
  (a) Water bag must be clear.
  (b) Water will taste like the plant smells.

Figure VII-10. Transpiration Bag

24

3. **Water Preparation and Storage**
    a. Filtration:
        (1) Seepage basin (see Figure VII-11).
        (2) Filter through porous material (sand/charcoal).

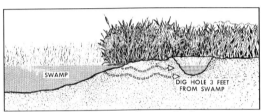

Figure VII-11. Seepage Basin

    b. Purification:
        (1) Water from live plants requires no further treatment.
        (2) Purify all other water:
            (a) Boil at least one minute.
            (b) To improve taste, pour from one container to another to aerate.
            (c) Water purification tablets. Follow instructions.
    c. Potable Water:
        (1) If water cannot be purified, obtain water from a clear, cold, clean, and fast running source (if possible).
        (2) Put in clear container and expose to the sun's ultraviolet rays to kill bacteria.
    d. Storage. To prevent contamination, use a clean, covered or sealed container:
        (1) Trash bag.
        (2) Prophylactic.
        (3) Section of bamboo.
        (4) Flotation gear.

Chapter IV
FOOD

1. **Food Procurement**
    a. Locating:
        (1) Mammals:
            (a) Trails lead to watering, feeding, and bedding areas.
            (b) Look for fresh droppings or tracks.
        (2) Birds:
            (a) Observing the direction of flight in the early morning and late afternoon may lead to feeding, watering, and roosting areas.
            (b) The noise of birds may indicate nesting areas.
        (3) Fish and other marine life:
            (a) Streams and rivers (see Figure VIII-1).
            (b) Lakes, ponds and oceans.
            (c) Along shores.

1   OVERHANGING BRUSH
2   UNDERCUT
3   POOL FROM BACKWASH
4   FEEDER STREAM
5   BEHIND ROCKS
6   FALLEN TREE

Figure VIII-1. Fishing Locations

        (4) Reptiles and amphibians are found almost worldwide.

        (5) Insects may be found:
            (a) In dead logs and stumps.
            (b) Ant and termite mounds.
            (c) On ponds, lakes, and slow moving streams.
    b. Procurement techniques:
        (1) Snares:
            (a) Work while unattended.
            (b) Location of snares:
                • Trails leading to water, feeding, and bedding areas.
                • The mouth of dens (see Figure VIII-2).

26

Figure VIII-2. Snare Placement

(c) Construction of simple loop snare:
- Use materials that will not break under the strain of holding an animal.
- Use a figure eight (locking loop) if wire is used, (see Figure VIII-3).

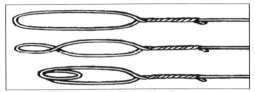
Figure VIII-3. Locking Loop

- Once tightened, the wire locks in place, preventing reopening, and the animal's escape.
- To construct a squirrel pole (see Figure VIII-4) use simple loop snares.

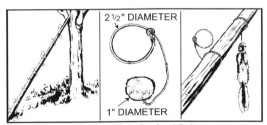
Figure VIII-4. Squirrel Pole

- Make noose opening slightly larger than the animal's head, three-finger width for squirrels, fist-sized for rabbits.

(d) Placement of snares:

27

- Avoid disturbing the area.
- Use funneling (natural or improvised) (see Figure VIII-5).
- Set as many snares as possible.

(2) A noose stick is easier and safer to use than the hands.

Figure VIII-5. Funneling

(3) Twist stick (see Figure VIII-6):
  (a) Insert forked stick into a den until something soft is met.
  (b) Twist the stick, binding the animal's hide in the fork.
  (c) Remove the animal from the den.
  (d) Be ready to kill the animal, it may be dangerous.

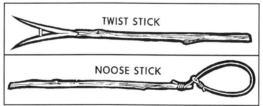

Figure VIII-6. Procurement Devices

(4) Hunting and fishing devices:
  (a) Club or rock.
  (b) Spear.
  (c) Slingshot.
  (d) Pole, line, and hook.
  (e) Net.
  (f) Trap.
(5) Fishing traps and devices (see Figure VIII-7).

28

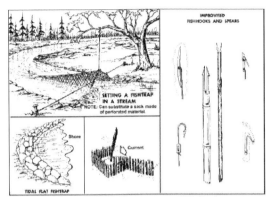

Figure VIII-7. Procurement Methods

(6) Precautions:

    (a) Wear shoes to protect the feet when wading in water.

    (b) Avoid reaching into dark holes.

    (c) Animals in distress may attract the enemy.

    (d) Kill animals prior to handling.

    (e) Do not secure fishing lines to yourself or the raft.

    (f) Kill fish before bringing them into the raft.

    (g) Do not eat fish with:

        • Spines.

        • Unpleasant odor.

        • Pale, slimy gills.

        • Sunken eyes.

        • Flabby skin.

        • Flesh that remains dented when pressed.

    (h) Do not eat fish eggs or liver (entrails).

    (i) Avoid all crustaceans above the high tide mark.

    (j) Avoid cone-shaped shells. (See figure VIII-8).

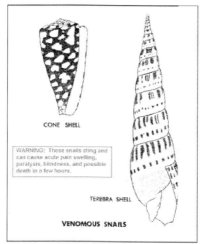

Figure VIII-8. Cone-shaped shells

(k) Avoid hairy insects, the hairs could cause irritation or infection.
(l) Avoid poisonous insects, for example:
  • Centipedes.
  • Scorpions.
  • Poi_ _ _ _ _ _ _ _piders.
(m) Avoid disease carrying insects, such as:
  • Flies.
  • Mosquitoes.
  • Ticks.
c. Plant Foods (Before using the following guide use your evasion chart to identify edible plants):

Note: If you cannot positively identify an edible plant and must use an unknown plant, these guidelines may help you determine edibility.

(1) Selection Criteria:
  (a) Before testing for edibility, ensure there are enough plants to make testing worth your time and effort. Each part of a plant (roots, leaves, stems, bark, etc.) requires more than 24 hours to test. Do not waste time testing a plant that is not abundant.
  (b) Test only one part of one plant at a time.
  (c) Remember that eating large portions of plant food on an empty stomach may cause diarrhea, nausea, or cramps. Two good examples of this are such familiar foods as green apples and wild onions. Even after testing food and finding it safe, eat in moderation.

30

(2) Avoid plants with the following characteristics:

    (a) Milky sap (Dandelion has milky sap but is safe to eat and easily recognizable).
    (b) Spines, fine hairs and thorns (skin irritants/contact dermatitis), (Prickly pear and thistles are exceptions. Bracken fern fiddleheads also violate this guideline).
    (c) Mushrooms and fungus.
    (d) Umbrella shaped flowers (Hemlock is eliminated).
    (e) Bulbs (Onions are the only thing that smell like onions).
    (f) Grain heads with pink, purplish or black spurs.
    (g) Beans bulbs or seeds inside pods.
    (h) Old or wilted leaves.
    (i) Plants with shiny leaves.
    (j) White and yellow berries (Aggregate berries such as black and dewberries are always edible, test all others before eating).
    (k) Almond scent in woody parts and leaves.

d. Test Procedures:

    (1) Test only one part of a plant at a time.
    (2) Separate the plant into its basic components (Stems roots buds and flowers).
    (3) Smell the food for strong acid odors. Remember smell alone does not indicate a plant is edible or inedible.
    (4) Do not eat 8 hours prior to the test and drink only purified water.
    (5) During the 8 hours you abstain from eating test for contact poisoning by placing a piece of the plant on the inside of your elbow or wrist. The sap or juice should contact the skin. Usually 15 minutes is enough time to allow for a reaction.
    (6) During testing take nothing by mouth except purified water and the plant you are testing.
    (7) Select a small portion of a single part and prepare it the way you plan to eat it.
    (8) Before placing the prepared plant in your mouth, touch a small portion (a pinch) to the outer surface of you lip to test for burning or itching.
    (9) If after 3 minutes there is no reaction on your lip, place the plant on your tongue, and hold it for 15 minutes.
    (10) If there is no reaction, thoroughly chew a pinch and hold it in your mouth for 15 minutes. **DO NOT SWALLOW**. If any ill effects occur rinse out your mouth with water.

    (11) If nothing abnormal occurs swallow the food and wait 8 hours. If any ill effects occur during

this period, induce vomiting and drink a water and charcoal mixture.

(12) If no ill effects occur, eat ¼ cup of the same plant prepared the same way. Wait another 8 hours. If no ill effects occur, the plant part as prepared is safe for eating.

Notes:
1. Ripe tropical fruits should be peeled and eaten raw. If the fruit is soft, color does not always indicate ripeness. Cook unripe fruits and discard seeds and skin.
2. Cook underground portions if possible to reduce possible bacterial contamination and ease digestion of their generally high starch content.
3. During evasion you may not be able to cook. Concentrate your efforts on leafy green plants, ripe fruits and above ground ripe vegetables not requiring significant preparation.

---

2. **Food Preparation**
   a. Animal food gives the greatest food value per pound.
   b. Butchering and skinning:
      (1) Mammals:
         (a) Remove the skin and use for improvising.
         (b) Glove skinning.
         (c) One cut skinning of small game (see Figure VIII-9):

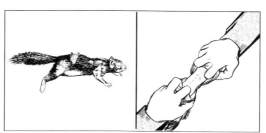

Figure VIII-9. Small Game Skinning

   • Open the abdominal cavity,
   • Avoid rupturing the intestines.
   • Remove the intestines.
   • Save inner organs (heart, liver, and kidneys) and all meaty parts of the skull, brain, tongue and eyes.
         (d) Wash when ready to use.
         (e) If preserving the meat, remove it from the bones.
      (2) Frogs and snakes:
         (a) Skin.
         (b) Discard skin, head w/2 inches of body, and internal organs.
      (3) Fish:
         (a) Scale (if necessary) and gut fish soon after procurement.

32

(b) Insert knifepoint into anus of fish and cut open the belly.

(c) Remove entrails.

(d) Remove gills to prevent spoilage.

(4) Birds:

 (a) Gut soon after killing.

 (b) Protect from flies.

 (c) You may skin or pluck birds.

 (d) Scavengers and sea birds should be skinned.

(5) Insects:

 (a) Remove all hard portions such as the legs of grasshoppers or crickets.

 (b) The rest is edible.

 (c) Recommend cooking grasshopper-size insects.

Note: Dead insects spoil rapidly, do not save.

---

(6) Fruits, berries, and most nuts can be eaten raw.

c. Cooking:

(1) Thoroughly cook all wild game, freshwater fish, clams, mussels, snails, crawfish, and scavenger birds to kill internal parasites.

(2) Saltwater fish may be eaten raw.

(3) Boiling is the most nutritious method of cooking, consume the broth:

 (a) Make metal cooking containers from ration cans.

 (b) Drop heated rocks into containers to boil water or cook food.

(4) Baking:

 (a) Wrap in leaves or pack in mud.

 (b) Bury food in dirt under coals of fire.

(5) Leaching. Some nuts (acorns) must be leached to remove the bitter taste of tannin. Use one of the following leaching methods:

 (a) First method:

  • Soaking and pouring the water off.

  • Crushing and pouring water through cold water should be tried first; however, boiling water is sometimes best.

  • Discard water.

 (b) Second method:

  • Boil, pour off water, and taste the plant.

  • If bitter, repeat process until palatable.

(6) Roasting:

 (a) Shake shelled nuts in a container with hot coals.

 (b) Roast thinly sliced meat and insects over a candle.

3. **Food Preservation**

a. Keeping an animal alive is one method of preserving it.

b. Refrigeration:

(1) Long term:

 (a) Food buried in snow maintains a temperature of approximately 32^0 F.

  (b) Frozen food will not decompose.

  (c) Freeze in meal-size portions.

 (2) Short term:

  (a) Food wrapped in waterproof material and placed in a stream remains cool in summer months.

  (b) Earth below the surface, particularly in shady areas or along streams, is cooler than the surface.

  (c) Wrap food in absorbent material such as cotton and re- wet as the water evaporates.

c. Drying and smoking removes moisture and preserves food:

 (1) Use salt, to improve flavor and promote drying.

 (2) Cut or pound meat into thin strips.

 (3) Remove fat.

 (4) Do not use pitch woods such as fir or pine, they produce soot giving the meat an undesirable taste.

d. Protecting meat from animals and insects:

 (1) Wrap food:

  (a) Use clean material.

  (b) Wrap pieces individually.

  (c) Assure all corners of the wrapping are insect proof.

 (2) Hanging meat:

  (a) Cover during daylight hours to protect from insects.

  (b) Hang meat in the shade.

 (3) Packing meat on the trail:

  (a) Wrap before flies appear in the morning.

  (b) Place meat in fabric or clothing for insulation.

  (c) Place meat inside the pack for carrying. Soft material acts as insulation helping keep the meat cool.

  (d) Carry shellfish, crabs, and shrimp in wet seaweed.

e. Wrap soft fruits and berries in leaves or moss.

f. Do not store food in the shelter, it attracts unwanted animals.

Chapter V
PERSONAL PROTECTION

1. **Priorities**
   a. Evaluate available resources and situation; accomplish individual tasks accordingly.
   b. First 24 hours in order of situational needs:
      (1) Construct survival shelter according to selection criteria.
      (2) Procure water.
      (3) Establish multiple survival signals.
      (4) Fire.
   c. Second 24 hours:
      (1) Construct necessary tools and weapons.
      (2) Procure food.

2. **Care and Use of Clothing**
   a. Never discard clothing.
   b. Wear loose and layered clothing:
      (1) Tight clothing restricts blood flow regulating body temperature.
      (2) Layers create more dead air space.
      (3) In hot areas keep entire body covered to prevent sunburn and dehydration.
   c. Avoid overheating:
      (1) Remove layers of clothing before strenuous activities.
      (2) When fully clothed, the majority of body heat escapes through the head and neck areas.
      (3) Use a hat to regulate body heat.
      (4) In hot environments, wear a hat when in direct sunlight.
   d. On the ocean in hot weather, dampen clothing:
      (1) Use salt water, not drinking water.
      (2) Dry clothing before dark to prevent hypothermia.
   e. Keep clothing dry to maintain its insulation qualities, dry damp clothing in the sun or by a fire.
   f. If you fall into the water in the winter:
      (1) Build fire.
      (2) Remove wet clothing and rewarm by fire.
      (3) Finish drying clothing by fire.
   g. If no fire is available:
      (1) Remove clothing and get into sleeping bag (if available).
      (2) Allow wet clothes to freeze.
      (3) Break ice out of clothing.
   h. Keep clothing clean, dirt reduces its insulation qualities:
      (1) Do not sit or lie directly on the ground.
      (2) Wash clothing whenever possible.
   i. Examine clothing frequently for damage, and repair when necessary using:
      (1) Needle and thread.
      (2) Safety pins.
      (3) Tape.
   j. Improvised foot protection (see Figure VI-1):

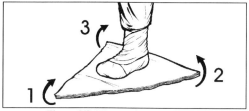

Figure VI-1 Improvised Foot Wear

(1) Cut two to four layers of cloth into a 30-inch square.

(2) Fold into a triangle.

(3) Center foot on triangle with toes toward corner.

(4) Fold front over the toes.

(5) Fold side corners, one at a time, over the instep.

(6) Secure by rope, vines, tape etc, or tuck into other layers of material.

2. Other Protective Equipment

k. Sleeping bag:

(1) Fluff before use especially at foot of bag.

(2) Air and dry daily to remove body moisture.

(3) May be improvised with available material, dry grass, leaves, dry moss, etc.

l. Sun and snow goggles (see Figure VI-2):

IMPROVISED SUNSHADES

BARK

WEBBING

Figure VI-2. Sun and Snow Goggles

(1) Wear in bright sun or snow conditions.

(2) Improvise by cutting small horizontal slits in webbing or bark, or similar materials.

m. Gaiters (see Figure VI-3):

Figure VI-3. Gaiters

  (1) Used to protect from sand, snow, insects, and scratches.

  (2) Wrap material around lower leg and top of boots.

3. Shelters
  a. Evasion considerations apply.
  b. Site selection:
    (1) Near signal and recovery site.
    (2) Food and water available.
    (3) Avoid natural hazards:
      (a) Dead standing trees.
      (b) Drainage and dry river beds except in combat areas.
      (c) Avalanche areas.
    (4) Location large and level enough to lie down in.
  c. Types of shelters:
    (1) Find shelter requiring minimal improvements (see Figure VI-4).

Figure VI-4. Immediate Shelters

37

(a) In temperate climates, protection from wind and rain is sufficient.

(2) Cold climates (see Figures VI-5, 6, & 7):

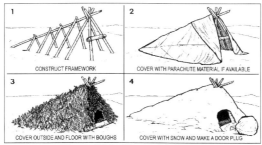

Figure VI-5. Thermal A Frame

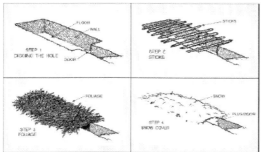

Figure VI-6. Snow Trench

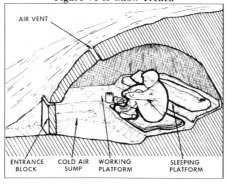

Figure VI-7. Snow Cave

(a) An enclosed, insulated shelter may be required.
(b) Snow is the most abundant insulating material.
(c) An air vent is required to prevent carbon monoxide poisoning when using an open flame inside enclosed shelters.
(d) As a general rule, unless you can see your breath – your snow shelter is too warm and should be cooled down to preclude melting and dripping.

(3) Hot climates (see Figure VI-8):
(a) A shade shelter is required to protect from UV rays.
(b) The shelter floor should be elevated or dug down (approximately 18 inches) to reduce the surface temperature.
(c) For thermal protection, a minimum of two layers of material suspended 12-18 inches above the head is required.
(d) White is the best color to reflect heat (inner most layer should be of darker material).

Figure VI-8. Poncho / Parachute Shade Shelter

(4) Tropical/wet climate (see Figure VI-9 & 10). An enclosed, elevated shelter is needed for protection from dampness and. insects.

d. Shelter construction:
(1) Entrance 45-90^0 from prevailing wind.
(2) Cover with available material.
(3) If natural materials are used, arrange them in layers starting at the bottom with each layer overlapping the previous one.
(4) If using porous material, like a, parachute, blankets, etc.:
(a) Stretch as tight as possible.
(b) Use a 40^0–60^0 slope.
(c) Use additional layers in heavy rains.

e. Shelter construction materials:
(1) Raft and raft parts.
(2) Vehicle or aircraft parts.
(3) Blankets, poncho, or parachute material.
(4) Sheet of plastic or plastic bag.
(5) Bark peeled off dead trees.
(6) Boughs and broad leaves.
(7) Grass and sod.

(8) Snow.

(9) Sand and rocks.

f. Construct a bed to protect from cold, damp ground using:

(1) Raft or foam rubber from vehicle seats.

(2) Boughs, leaves, or dry moss.

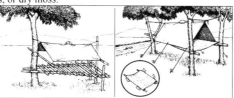

Figure VI-9. Raised Platform Shelter

Figure VI-10. Shingle Method

4. **Fire**

Note: Weigh hazards and risks of detection against the need for a fire.

a. Evasion considerations:

(1) Use trees or other source to dissipate smoke.

(2) Use fires at dusk, dawn or during inclement weather.

(3) Use fires at times when the local populace is cooking.

b. Fire building:

(1) The three essential elements for starting a fire are heat, fuel, and oxygen:

(2) Some heat sources to start fire are:

(a) Matches or lighter.

40

(b) Flint and steel (experiment with various rocks and metals until a good spark is produced).
(c) Sparks from batteries.
(d) Concentrated sunlight, use magnifying glass or flashlight reflectors.
(e) Pyrotechnics, such as flares (last resort), etc.
(f) Friction method (see Figure VI-11).

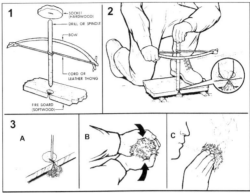

Figure VI-11. Friction Method

Note: If possible, carry a fire starting device with you.

c. Fuel is divided into three stages; tinder, kindling, and fuel:
(1) Gather large amounts of each stage before igniting the fire.
(2) Examples of tinder, the first stage, include:
   (a) Cotton.
   (b) Candle (shred the wick, not the wax).
   (c) Plastic spoon, fork, or knife.
   (d) Foam rubber.
   (e) Dry bark.
   (f) Dry grasses.
   (g) Gun powder.
   (h) Pitch.
   (i) Petroleum products.
(3) Tinder must be very finely shaved, or shredded, to provide a low combustion point and fluffed to allow oxygen to flow through. (To get tinder to burn hotter and longer, saturate ith Vaseline, Chapstick, insect repellant, aircraft fuel, etc.)
(4) Kindling, the second stage, must be small enough to ignite from the small flame of the tinder. Gradually add larger kindling until arriving at the size of fuel to burn.
(5) Examples of fuel, the third stage, include:
   (a) Dry hardwood—removing bark reduces smoke.
   (b) Bamboo—open chambers to prevent explosion.

(c) Dry dung.

d. Fires are built to meet specific needs or uses (see Figures VI-12, VI-13, VI-14 and VI-15).

Figure VI-12. Teepee Fire

Note: Use the Teepee Fire to produce a concentrated heat source for cooking, light, or signaling.

Figure VI-13. Log Cabin or Pyramid Fires

Note: Use the log cabin fire to produce large amounts of light and heat, to dry out wet wood, and provide coals for cooking, etc.

e. Use fire reflectors to get the most warmth from a fire. Build fires against rocks or logs (see Figure VI-14).

Note: Do not use porous rocks or riverbed rock—they may explode when heated.

Figure VI-14. Sod Fire and Reflector

Note: Use the Dakota fire hole for high winds or evasion situations.

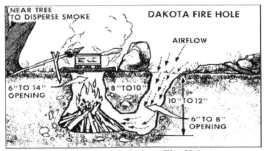

Figure VI-15. Dakota Fire Hole

f. Improvised stoves are very efficient (see Figure VI-16).

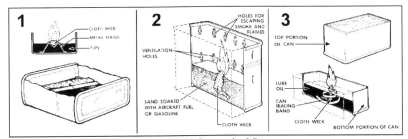

Figure VI-16. Improvised Stove

Chapter VI
RECOVERY OPERATIONS

1. **Responsibilities**
   a. Establish radio contact with recovery forces, if radio equipped.
   b. Maintain communication with recovery forces until recovered.
   c. Be prepared to authenticate IAW. Theater Communication Plan(TCP).
   d. Cross or reverse authenticate as required.
   e. Follow recovery force instructions, be prepared to report:
      (1) Enemy activity in the recovery area.
      (2) Recovery site characteristics (slope, obstacles, size, etc.).
      (3) Number in party / medical situation.
      (4) Signal devices available.
   f. If no radio, a ground-to-air signal may be your only means to effect recovery.

2. **Site Selection**
   a. Locate area for landing pick-up, if practical (approx. 150 feet diameter, free of obstructions, and if possible flat and level).
   b. Assess any evidence of human activity at or near the site.
   c. Locate several concealment sites around area.
   d. Plan several tactical entry and exit routes.

3. **Site Preparation**
   a. Pack and secure all equipment.
   b. Prepare signaling devices, (use as directed or as briefed).
   c. Mentally review recovery methods (aircraft, ground force, boat, etc.).

4. **Recovery Procedures**
   a. Assist recovery force in identifying your position.
   b. Stay concealed until recovery is imminent.
   c. For a landing/ground recovery:
      (1) Assume a non-threatening posture.
      (2) Secure weapons and avoid quick movement.
      (3) Do not approach recovery vehicle until instructed. Beware of rotors/propellers when approaching recovery vehicle, especially on sloping or uneven terrain.
   d. For hoist recovery devices (see Figures IV-1 and IV-2):
      (1) Let device contact the ground before touching to avoid static discharge.
      (2) Sit or kneel for stability while donning device.
      (3) Put safety strap under armpits.
      (4) Ensure cable is in front of you.
      (5) Keep hands clear of all hardware and connectors.
      (6) DO NOT become entangled in cable.

(7) Use a thumbs up, vigorous cable shake, or radio call to signal you are ready.

(8) Drag feet on the ground to decrease oscillation.

(9) Do not assist during hoist or when pulled into the rescue vehicle. Follow crewmember instructions.

e. For non-hoist recovery (rope or unfamiliar equipment):

(1) Create a "fixed loop" big enough to place under armpits (See Figure IV-3).

(2) Follow the procedures in "d" above.

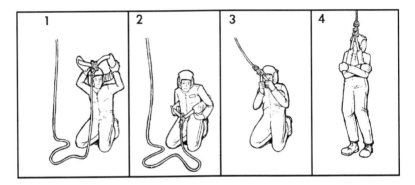

Figure IV–1. Rescue Strap

Figure IV-2. Forest Penetrator

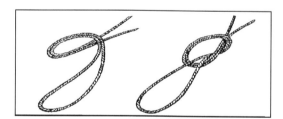

Figure IV–3. Fixed Loop

Chapter VII
RADIO COMMUNICATIONS AND SIGNALING

> **Note:** Inventory and review the operating instructions of all communications and signaling equipment.

1. **Radio communications (voice and data)**
   a. If you have a locator beacon, find it and turn it off - take it with you to supplement radio communications.
   b. Make initial contact ASAP or IAW theater communications plan (TCP).
   c. If no immediate contact, then follow TCP.
   d. Locate spare radio and batteries–keep warm and dry.
   e. Transmissions:
      (1) Use concealment sites that optimize line of sight.
      (2) Face recovery asset.
      (3) Keep antenna perpendicular to intended receiver (see Figure III-1).
      (4) Do not ground antenna (i.e. finger on antenna or attaching bolt, space blanket, vegetation etc).
      (5) Keep transmissions short (3-5 seconds maximum). Use data burst if available.
      (6) Move after each transmission if possible.
      (7) If transmitting in the blind, ensure a clear line of sight towards the equator.
   f. Listening—use published reception times in the TCP, or as directed by recovery forces.

2. **Signaling**
   a. Pyrotechnic signals:
      (1) Prepare early (weather permitting).
      (2) Use IAW TCP or as directed by recovery forces.
      (3) Extend over raft's edge prior to activating.
   b. Signal mirror (see Figure III-2):
      (1) Use as directed by recovery forces.
      (2) If no radio, use only with confirmed friendly forces.
      (3) Cover when not in use.

> **Note:** Make a mirror from any shiny metal or glass.

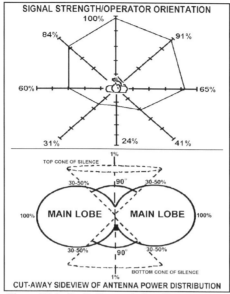

Figure III-1. Radio Transmission Characteristics

c. Strobe light:

  (1) Prepare filters and shield early.

  (2) Use IAW TCP or as directed by recovery forces.

  (3) Conserve battery life.

Note: Produces one residual flash when turned off.

Figure III-2. Sighting Techniques

d. Pattern signals–use published TCP signals:
  (1) Materials:
    (a) Manmade (space blanket, signal paulin, parachute).
    (b) Natural. Use materials that contrast the color and/or texture of the signaling area. (rocks, brush, branches, stomped grass).Location:
    (c) Maximize visibility from above.
    (d) Site should offer concealment from ground observation.
  (2) Size (large as possible) and ratio (see Figure III-3).
  (3) Shape—maintain straight lines and sharp corners.
  (4) Contrast—use color and shadows.
  (5) Pattern signals (see Figure III-4).
e. Sea dye marker:
  (1) Do not waste in rough seas or fast moving water.
  (2) Conserve unused dye by re-wrapping.
  (3) May be used to color snow.
f. Non-tactical considerations:
  (1) Use a fire at night.
  (2) Use smoke for day, (tires or petroleum products for dark smoke and green vegetation for light smoke, see Figure III- 5).
  (3) Use signal mirror to sweep horizon.
  (4) Audio signals (i.e., voice, whistle, and weapons fire).

Note: Any of the above signals used in a series of three, evenly spaced, is recognized as an international distress symbol

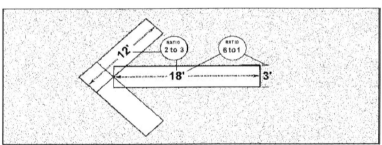

Figure III-3. Size and ratio

49

NO.	MESSAGE	CODE SYMBOL
1	REQUIRE ASSISTANCE	**V**
2	REQUIRE MEDICAL ASSISTANCE	**X**
3	NO or NEGATIVE	**N**
4	YES or AFFIRMATIVE	**Y**
5	PROCEEDING IN THIS DIRECTION	**↑**

Figure III-4. Signal Key

LOTS OF DEAD DRY TWIGS OR KINDLING FOR QUICK STARTING FAST-BURNING FIRE

EVERGREEN BOUGHS

SMALL OPENING FOR LIGHTING FIRE

Figure III-5. Smoke Generator

Chapter VIII
NAVIGATION

Note: Assess the threat and apply appropriate evasion principles.

1. **Stay or Move**
   a. Stay with the vehicle/aircraft in a permissive environment.
   b. Leave only when:
      (1) Dictated by the threat.
      (2) Certain of location, have a known destination, and the ability to get there.
      (3) Water, food, shelter, and (or) help can be reached.
      (4) Convinced rescue is not coming.
   c. If you decide to travel, consider the following:
      (1) Follow briefed evasion plan.
      (2) Which direction to travel and why.
      (3) What equipment to take, cache, or destroy.
   d. Leave information at your start point (only in permissive environment):
      (1) Destination.
      (2) Route of travel.
      (3) Personal condition.
      (4) Supplies available.
   e. Evasion considerations:
      (1) Do not write on the map.
      (2) Do not soil the map by touching the destination.
      (3) Do not fold in a manner providing travel information.

2. **Navigation and Position Determination**
   a. Determine your general location:
      (1) Develop a working knowledge of operational area:
         (a) Natural geographic checkpoints.
         (b) Manmade checkpoints.
         (c) Use the "Rate x Time = Distance" formula.
      (2) Use previous knowledge of operational area.
      (3) Use information provided in the map legend.
      (4) Use prominent landmarks.
      (5) Visualize map to determine position.
   b. Determine cardinal directions (north, south, east, and west):
      (1) Use compass.

Note: Margin of error increases the closer you are to the Equator for the following methods.

   (2) Stick and shadow method determines a true north-south line (see Figure II-1).

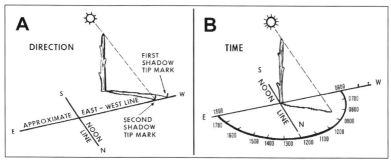

Figure II-1. Stick and Shadow Method

(3) Sunrise/moonrise in the east, sun/moonset in the west.

(4) Use a wristwatch to determine cardinal direction (see Figure II-2): (Use this method for general direction only.)

    (a) Digital watches may be used, visualize a clock face on the watch.

    (b) Northern Hemisphere, Point hour hand at the sun. South is half way between the hour hand and 12 o'clock position.

    (c) Southern Hemisphere, Point the 12 o'clock position on your watch at the sun. North is half way between the 12 o'clock position and the hour hand.

(5) Pocket Navigator (see Figure II-3):

    (a) Gather necessary materials:

        • Paper or other flat writing material (e.g. MRE box).

        • 1-2" shadow tip device (e.g. twig, nail, match).

        • Pen or pencil.

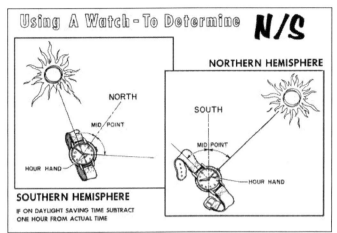

Figure II-2. Direction Using a Watch

(b) Construction (start at sunup; end at sundown):
- Attach shadow tip device in center of paper.
- Place and secure navigator on flat surface (do not move during set up period).
- Mark tip of shadow every 30 minutes and annotate time.
- Connect marks to form an arc.
- The shortest line between base of shadow tip device and curved line is a north-south line.
- Indicate north with a drawn arrow.

(c) Use during travel:
- Hold navigator so the shadow aligns with mark of present time.
- Drawn arrow now points to true north.

Navigator is current for approximately one week.

Note: The Pocket Navigator is not recommended if evading.

(6) Stars (see Figure II-4):
  (a) Use North Star to locate true north-south line.
  (b) Use Southern Cross to locate true north-south line.

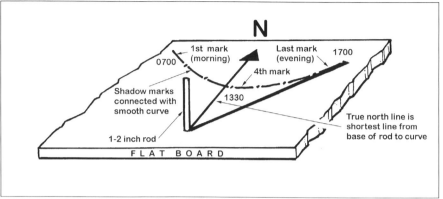

Figure II-3 Pocket Navigator

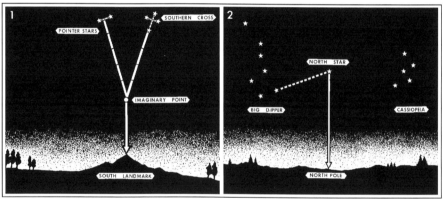

Figure II-4. Stars

c. Orient the map:

  (1) Orienting a map using a true north-south line (see Figure II- 5):

    (a) Unfold map and place on a firm, flat, level non-metallic surface.

    (b) Align the compass on a true north-south line.

    (c) Rotate map and compass until stationary index line aligns with the magnetic variation indicated in marginal information:

      • Easterly, subtract variation from 360^0.

      • Westerly, add variation to 360^0.

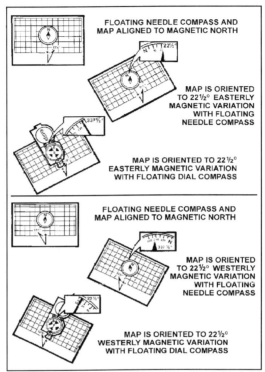

Figure II-5. Orienting a Map Using a True North-South Line

(2) Orienting map with a compass rose (see Figure II-6):

    (a) Place edge of the lensatic compass on magnetic north line of the compass rose closest to your location.

    (b) Rotate map and compass until compass reads 360°.

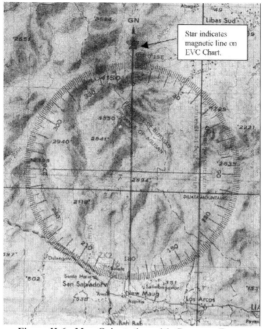

Figure II-6. Map Orientation with Compass Rose

(3) No compass; orient map using cardinal direction obtained by the stick and shadow method, or the celestial aids (stars) method.

d. Determine specific location:

  (1) Global Positioning System (GPS):

    (a) Do not use GPS for primary navigation.

    (b) Use GPS only to confirm your position.

    (c) Select area providing maximum satellite reception.

    (d) Conserve GPS battery life.

  (2) Triangulation (resection) with a compass (see Figure II-7):

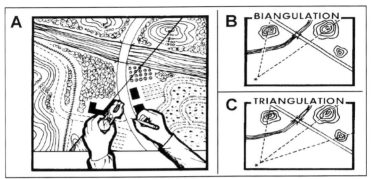

Figure II-7. Triangulation

(a) Try to use three or more azimuths.

(b) Positively identify a major land feature and determine a line of position (LOP) (see figure II-7a).

(c) Each time compass is used, check map orientation.

(d) Plot the LOP using a thin stick, blade of grass or pencil (non-tactical).

(e) Repeat steps b through d for other LOPs.

e. Use the compass for night navigation:

(1) Set up compass for night navigation (see Figure II-8).

(2) Align north-seeking arrow with luminous line and follow front of compass.

(3) Use point to point navigation.

f. Route selection techniques:

(1) Circumnavigation:

(a) Find a prominent landmark on the opposite side of the obstacle.

(b) Contour around obstacle to landmark.

(c) Resume your route of travel.

57

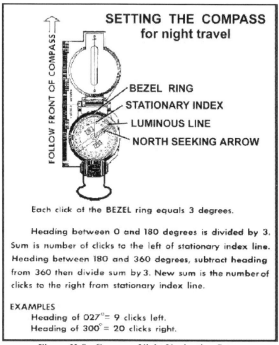

Figure II-8. Compass Night Navigation Setup

(2) Dogleg and 90 degree offset. (See Figure II-9).

(3) Straight-line heading:

   (a) Maintain heading until reaching destination.

   (b) Open terrain, 1200 paces per mile (average) or 600 per kilometer (60 per 100 meters).

   (c) Rough terrain, 1800 paces per mile (average) or 900 per kilometer (90 per 100 meters).

   (d) One pace is every time the same foot touches ground.

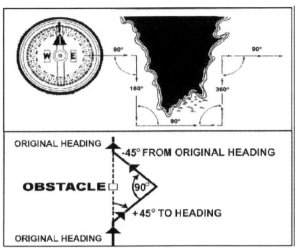
Figure II-9. Dogleg and 90 degree offset

    (4) Deliberate offset:
        (a) Used when finding a point on a linear feature (i.e. road or river).
        (b) Intentionally navigate to left or right of target so you know which way to turn at the linear feature.
    (5) Point-to-point:
        (a) Same as straight line.
        (b) Pick out landmarks on the heading and walk the trail of least resistance to a point.
        (c) On reaching a point, establish another landmark and continue.

3. **Travel**
    a. Pick the easiest and safest route (unless evading).
    b. Maintain a realistic pace. Take rest stops when needed.
    c. Avoid overdressing and overheating.
    d. Consider food and water requirements.
    e. Take special care of feet.
    f. Pack equipment to prevent loss, damage, pack imbalance, and personal safety.
    g. Go around obstacles, not over or through them.
    h. Travel on trails whenever possible (non-tactical).
    i. Travel in forested areas if possible.
    j. Avoid creek bottoms and ravines with no escape in case of heavy rains.
    k. Swamps, lakes and unfordable rivers:
        (1) Swamps, lakes, and bogs may have to be circumnavigated.
        (2) Travel downstream to find people and slower water.

(3) Travel upstream to find narrower and shallow water.

4. **River Travel**
   a. River travel may be faster and save energy when hypothermia is not a factor. May be a primary mode of travel and LOC in a tropical environment, use with caution if evading.
   b. In shallow water, use a pole to move the raft.
   c. In deep water, use an oar.
   d. Stay near inside edge of river bends (current speed is less).
   e. Keep near shore.
   f. Watch for *dangers*:
      (1) Snags.
      (2) Sweepers (overhanging limbs and trees).
      (3) Rapids.
      (4) Waterfalls.
   g. Do not attempt to shoot the rapids.
   h. When crossing a river or large/deep stream, use a raft.
   i. Consider water depth before crossing without a flotation device.

5. **Ice and Snow**
   a. Travel should be limited to areas free of hazards.
   b. Do not travel in:
      (1) Blizzards.
      (2) Bitterly cold winds.
      (3) Poor visibility.
   c. Obstacles to winter travel:
      (1) Be aware of reduced daylight hours.
      (2) Deep soft snow; if movement is necessary, make snowshoes (see Figure II-10).

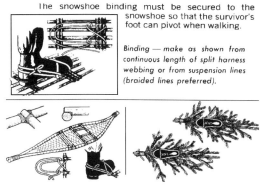

The snowshoe binding must be secured to the snowshoe so that the survivor's foot can pivot when walking.

Binding — make as shown from continuous length of split harness webbing or from suspension lines (braided lines preferred).

Figure II-10. Improvised Snowshoes

    (3) Travel is easier in early morning or late afternoon near dusk when snow is frozen or crusted.
    (4) Avoid avalanche prone areas:
       (a) Slopes 30-45 degrees or greater.
       (b) Trees devoid of uphill branches (identifies prior avalanches).
       (c) Heavy snow loading on ridge tops.
    (5) If caught in an avalanche:
       (a) Backstroke to decrease burial depth.
       (b) As snow slows down move hands around face to create air pocket.
    (6) Frozen water crossings:
       (a) Weak ice should be expected where:
         • Rivers are straight.
         • Objects protrude through ice.
         • Snow banks extend over the ice.
         • Rivers or streams come together.
         • Rising water vapor indicates open or warm areas.
       (b) Air pockets form when a frozen river loses volume.
  d. When crossing, distribute your weight by laying flat, belly crawling, or using snowshoes.
  e. Glacier travel is hazardous and should be avoided.

6. Mountainous Hazards
  a. Avoid ridge tops during storms (lightning hazard).
  b. Rock avalanches and mudslides.
  c. Avoid low areas (flash flood hazard).

7. Summer Harzards
    (1) Dense brush:
       (a) Travel on trails when possible (non-tactical).
       (b) Travel in forested areas if possible.
       (c) Avoid creek bottoms and ravines with no escape in case of heavy rains.
    (2) Swamps, lakes and unfordable rivers:
       (a) Swamps, lakes, and bogs may have to be circumnavigated.
       (b) Travel downstream to find people and slower water.
       (c) Travel upstream to find narrower and shallow water.

8. Dry Climates
  a. Do not travel unless certain of reaching the destination using the water supply available.
  b. When the days are hot, travel at dawn or dusk.
  c. Follow the easiest trail possible (non-tactical), avoiding:
    (1) Deep sandy dune areas.
    (2) Rough terrain.
  d. If a sandstorm occurs:
    (1) Mark your direction of travel.
    (2) Sit or lie down in direction of travel.
    (3) Try to get to the downwind side of natural shelter.

(4) Cover the mouth and nose with a piece of cloth.

(5) Protect the eyes.

(6) Remain stationary until the storm is over.

e. In sand dune areas:

(1) Follow hard valley floor between dunes.

(2) Travel on the windward side of dune ridges.

9. **Tropical Climates**

a. Travel only when it is light.

b. Avoid obstacles like thickets and swamps.

c. Part the vegetation to pass through.

d. Do not climb over logs if you can go around them.

e. Avoid grabbing vegetation, it may have spines or thorns (use gloves if possible).

f. Find trails:

(1) Where two streams meet.

(2) Where a low pass goes over a range of hills.

g. While traveling trails:

(1) Do not follow closed trails, they may lead to animal traps.

(2) Watch for disturbed areas on game trails, they may indicate a pitfall or trap.

(3) Do not sleep on a game trail.

(4) Use a walking stick to probe for pitfalls or traps.

10. **Open Seas**

a. Use of currents:

(1) Deploy sea anchor (see Figure II-11). Sea anchor may be adjusted to make use of existing currents.

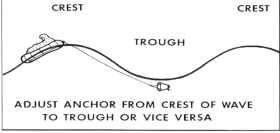

Figure II-11. Sea Anchor Deployment

(2) Sit low in the raft.

(3) Deflate the raft slightly so it rides lower in the water.

b. Use of winds:

(1) Pull in sea anchor.

(2) Inflate raft so it rides higher.

(3) Sit up in raft so body catches the wind.

(4) Construct a shade cover/sail (see Figure II-12).

(5) Sail aids in making landfall.

c. Making landfall:

(1) Indications of land:

(a) Fixed cumulus clouds in a clear sky or in a cloudy sky where all other clouds are moving.

(b) In the tropics, a greenish tint in the sky.

(c) In the arctic, a lighter colored reflection on clouds (open water causes dark gray reflections).

(d) Lighter colored water indicates shallow water.

(e) Land may be detected by odors and sounds:

• Odors from swamps and smoke.

• Roar of surf / bird cries coming from one direction.

(f) Directions from which birds fly at dawn and to which they fly at dusk.

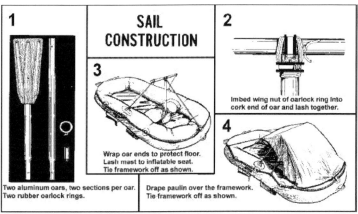

Figure II-12. Shade/ Sail Construction

d. Swimming ashore:

(1) Consider physical condition.

(2) Use a flotation aid.

(3) Secure all gear to body before beginning landfall.

(4) Remain in raft as long as possible.

(5) Try to make landfall during the lull between the sets of waves (waves are generally in sets of 7, from smallest to largest).

(6) Wear footgear and at least one layer of clothing.

(7) If thrown from raft, the sidestroke or breaststroke conserves strength.

(8) Moderate surf:

(a) Swim forward on the back of a wave.

  (b) Make a shallow dive just before the wave breaks to end the ride.
 (9) High surf:
  (a) Swim shoreward in the trough between waves.
  (b) When the seaward wave approaches, face it and submerge.
  (c) After it passes, work shoreward in the next trough.
 (10) If caught in the undertow of a large wave:
  (a) Remain calm and swim to the surface.
  (b) Lie as close to the surface as possible.
  (c) Parallel shoreline and attempt landfall at a point further down shore.
e. Selecting a landing point:
 (1) Avoid places where waves explode upon rocks.
 (2) If you land on rocky shores, find a place where waves rush up onto the rocks.
f. After selecting a landing site:
 (1) Face shoreward.
 (2) Assume a sitting position with feet two or three feet lower than head to absorb the shock of hitting submerged objects.
g. Rafting ashore:
 (1) Select landing point carefully.
 (2) Use caution landing when the sun is low and straight in front of you causing poor visibility.
 (3) If possible, land on the lee (downwind) side of islands or point of land.
 (4) Head for gaps in the surf line.
 (5) When going through surf:
  (a) Take down most shade/sails.
  (b) Use paddles to maintain control.
  (c) Deploy a sea anchor for stability.

Caution: Do not deploy a sea anchor if traveling through coral.

h. Make sea ice landings on large stable ice flows.
i. Icebergs, small flows, and disintegrating flows are dangerous:
 (1) Ice can cut a raft.
 (2) Use paddles to avoid sharp edges.
 (3) Store raft away from the ice edge.

Chapter IX
EVASION

1. **Planning**
   a. Review/Perform Quick Reference Checklist on inside cover.
   b. Evasion is a duty of all Service members. Guidelines for successful evasion include:
      (1) A positive attitude.
      (2) Use established procedures.
      (3) Follow your evasion plan of action.
      (4) Be patient and flexible. Flexibility is one of the most important keys to successful evasion. The evader is primarily interested in avoiding detection. Remember that people catch people. If the evader avoids detection, success is almost assured.
      (5) Drink water. Do not eat food without water.
      (6) Conserve strength for critical periods.
      (7) Rest and sleep as much as possible.
      (8) Stay out of sight.
   c. The following odors stand out and may give an evader away:
      (1) Scented soaps and shampoos.
      (2) Shaving cream, after-shave lotion, or other cosmetics.
      (3) Insect repellent — camouflage stick is least scented.
      (4) Gum and candy — have strong or sweet smell.
      (5) Tobacco—the odor is unmistakable.
   d. Where to go? Initiate evasion plan of action.
      (1) Near a suitable area for recovery.
      (2) Selected area for evasion (SAFE).
      (3) To a neutral or friendly country or area.
      (4) Designated area for recovery (DAR).

2. **Camouflage**
   a. Basic principles:
      (1) Disturb the area as little as possible.
      (2) Avoid activity that reveals movement to the enemy.
      (3) Apply personal camouflage.
   b. Use camouflage patterns (see Figure I-1):
      (1) Blotch pattern:
         (a) Temperate deciduous (leaf shedding) areas.
         (b) Desert areas (barren).
         (c) Barren snow.
      (2) Slash pattern:
         (a) Coniferous (evergreen) areas—broad slashes.
         (b) Jungle areas—broad slashes.
         (c) Grass—narrow slashes.
      (3) May use a combination of both.

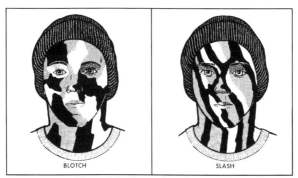

BLOTCH   SLASH

Figure I-1. Camouflage Patterns

c. Camouflage application:

(1) Face. Use dark colors on high spots and light colors on the remaining exposed areas (mask, netting, or hat help).

(2) Ears. The insides and the backs should have two colors to break up outlines.

(3) Head, neck (do not forget), and under chin. Use scarf, collar, vegetation, netting, or coloration methods.

(4) Give special attention to conceal light colored hair with a scarf or mosquito head net.

(5) Do not overlook hands, ears, neck, and body.

(6) Avoid unnecessary movement.

(7) Take advantage of natural concealment:

(a) Remember, foliage fades and wilts, change regularly.

(b) Change camouflage depending on the surroundings.

(c) Do not select all items from same source.

(d) Use stains from grasses, berries, dirt, and charcoal.

(8) Do not **over** camouflage.

(9) Remember when using shadows, they shift with the sun.

(10) Never expose shiny objects (i.e., watch, glasses, pens).

(11) Ensure watch alarms and hourly chimes are turned off.

(12) Remove unit patches, name tags, rank etc.

(13) Break up the outline of the body; "V" of crotch / armpits.

(14) When observing an area, do it from a prone and concealed position.

3. **Shelters**
   a. Use camouflage and concealment.
   b. Locate carefully:
      (1) Easy to remember acronym: **BLISS.**

B – **B**lend
L - **L**ow silhouette
I - **I**rregular shape
S – **S**mall
S – **S**ecluded location

      (2) Choose area:
         (a) Least likely to be searched (drainage's, rough terrain, military crest, etc.) and blends with the environment.
         (b) With escape routes.
         (c) With observable approaches – do not corner yourself.
      (3) Be wary of flash floods in ravines and canyons.
      (4) Concealment with minimal to no preparation.
      (5) Select natural concealment area.
      (6) Consider direction finding (DF) when transmitting from shelter.
      (7) Locate entrances / exits in brush and along ridges, ditches, and rocks to keep from forming paths to site.
      (8) Ensure overhead concealment.

4. **Movement**
   a. A moving object is easy to spot. If travel is necessary:
      (1) Mask with natural cover (see Figure I-2).
      (2) Use the military crest.
      (3) Restrict to periods of low light, bad weather, wind, or reduced enemy activity.

Figure I-2. Ground Movement

(4) Avoid silhouetting (see Figure I-3).
(5) Sporadic—every five to ten paces:
  (a) **STOP** at a point of concealment.
  (b) **LOOK** for signs of human or animal activity; (smoke, tracks, roads, troops, vehicles, aircraft, wire, buildings, etc). Watch for trip wires or booby traps and avoid leaving evidence of travel. Peripheral vision is more effective for recognizing movement at night and twilight.

Figure I-3. Avoid Silhouetting

      (c) **LISTEN** for vehicles, troops, aircraft, weapons, animals, etc.

      (d) **SMELL** for vehicles, troops, animals, etc.

   (6) Employ noise discipline, consider clothing and equipment.

b. An important factor is breaking up the human shape or lines that are recognizable at a distance.

c. Route selection requires detailed planning and special techniques (irregular route / zigzag) to camouflage evidence of travel.

d. Some techniques for concealing evidence of travel are:

   (1) Avoid disturbing the vegetation above knee level.

   (2) Do not break branches, leaves, or grass.

   (3) Use a walking stick to part vegetation and push it back to its original position.

   (4) Do not grab small trees or brush. This may scuff the bark, and create movement that is easily spotted. In snow country, this creates a path of snowless vegetation revealing your route.

   (5) Pick firm footing, carefully place the foot lightly, but squarely on the surface avoiding:

      (a) Overturning ground cover, rocks, and sticks.

      (b) Scuffing bark on logs and sticks.

      (c) Making noise by breaking sticks (cloth wrapped around feet helps muffle this).

      (d) Slipping.

      (e) Mangling of low grass and bushes that would normally spring back.

   (6) When tracks are unavoidable in soft footing, mask by:

      (a) Placing track in the shadows of vegetation, downed logs, and snowdrifts.

      (b) Moving before and during precipitation allows tracks to fill in.

      (c) Traveling during windy periods.

      (d) Taking advantage of solid surfaces (logs, rocks, etc.) leaving less evidence of travel.

      (e) Brushing or patting out tracks lightly to speed their breakdown or make them look old.

(7) Do not litter. Trash or lost equipment identifies who lost it. Secure everything, hide, or bury discarded items.

(8) If pursued by dogs, concentrate on defeating dog handler.

e. Obstacle penetration:

(1) Enter deep ditches feet first to avoid injury.

(2) Go around chain-link and wire fences. Go under if unavoidable.

(3) Penetrate rail fences, passing under or between lower rails. If impractical, go over the top, presenting as low a silhouette as possible (see Figure I-4).

(4) Cross roads after observation from concealment to determine enemy activity. Cross at points offering the best cover such as bushes, shadows, bend in road, etc. Cross in a manner leaving your footprints parallel (cross stepping sideways) to the road. (see Figure I-5).

Observe railroad tracks just like roads. Then align body parallel to tracks and face down, cross tracks, using a semi-pushup motion; repeat for second track (see Figure I-6).

Figure I-4. Rail Fences

Figure I-5. Road Crossing

70

Figure I-6. Railroad Tracks

WARNING
If three rails exist, one may be electrified.

Chapter X
MEDICAL

WARNING
These emergency medical procedures are for survival situations. Obtain professional medical treatment as soon as possible.

---

1. **Immediate First Aid Actions**
   a. Determine responsiveness:
      (1) If unconscious, arouse by shaking gently and shouting.
      (2) If no response:
         (a) Keep head and neck aligned with body.
         (b) Roll victim onto their back.
         (c) Open the airway by lifting the chin (see Figure V-1).
         (d) Look, listen and feel for air exchange.

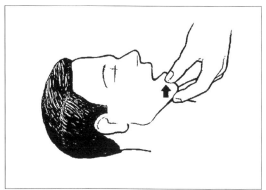

Figure V-1. Chin Lift

      (3) If victim is not breathing:
         (a) Cover victim's mouth with your own.
         (b) Pinch victims nostrils closed.
         (c) Fill victim's lungs with 2 slow breaths.
         (d) If breaths blocked, reposition airway; try again.
         (e) If breaths still blocked, give 5 abdominal thrusts:
            • Straddle the victim.
            • Place a fist between breastbone and belly button.
            • Thrust upward to expel air from stomach.
         (f) Sweep with finger to clear mouth.
         (g) Try 2 slow breaths again.
         (h) If the airway is still blocked, continue (c) through (f) until successful or exhausted.

(i) With open airway, give mouth to mouth breathing:
- One breathe every 5 seconds.
- Check for chest rise each time.

(4) If victim is unconscious, but breathing:
  (a) Keep head and neck aligned with body.
  (b) Roll victim on side (drains the mouth and prevents the tongue from blocking airway).

CAUTION: Do not remove an impaled object unless it interferes with the airway. You may cause more tissue damage and increase bleeding. For travel, you may shorten and secure the object.

b. Control bleeding:
  (1) Apply a pressure dressing (see Figure V-2).
  (2) If still bleeding:
    (a) Use direct pressure over the wound.
    (b) Elevate the wounded area above the heart.
  (3) If **still** bleeding:
    (a) Use a pressure point between the injury and the heart (see Figure V-3).
    (b) Maintain pressure for 6 to 10 minutes before checking to see if bleeding has stopped.
  (4) **If a limb wound is STILL bleeding:**

CAUTION: Use of a tourniquet is a LAST RESORT measure. Use only when severe, uncontrolled bleeding will cause loss of life. Recognize that long-term use of a tourniquet may cause loss of limb.

  (a) Apply tourniquet just above bleeding site on limb (see Figure V-4).
  (b) A band at least 3 inches (7.5 cm) wide is best.
  (c) Wrap band twice around the limb.
  (d) Tighten with a stick at least 6 inches (15 cm) long.
  (e) Tighten only enough to stop bleeding.
  (f) Note the time of application.
  (g) Do not cover the tourniquet.
  (h) Mark a "TK" on the forehead.

NOTE: The following directions apply **ONLY** in survival situations where rescue is unlikely and no medical aid is available.

  (i) If no rescue or medical aid is likely for over 2 hours, an attempt to **SLOWLY** loosen the tourniquet may be made 20 minutes after it is applied:
  - Ensure pressure dressing is in place.
  - Ensure bleeding has stopped
  - Loosen tourniquet SLOWLY to restore circulation.
  - Leave loosened tourniquet in position in case bleeding resumes.

c. Treat chest injuries:
  (1) Sucking chest wound:
    (a) Occurs when chest wall is penetrated.

(b) May cause victim to gasp for breath.

(c) May cause sucking sounds.

(d) May create bloody froth as air escapes the chest.

(2) Immediately seal wound with hand or airtight material.

(3) Tape airtight material (if available) over wound on three sides only:

(a) This dressing should create a one-way valve and allow air to escape from the wound but not to enter (see Figure V-5).

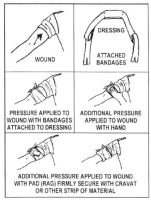

Figure V-2. Application of a Pressure Dressing

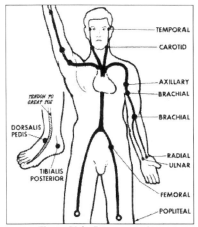

Figure V-3. Pressure Points

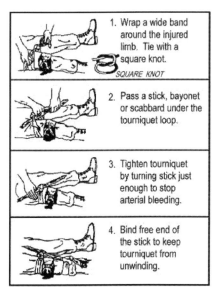

Figure V-4. Application of a Tourniquet

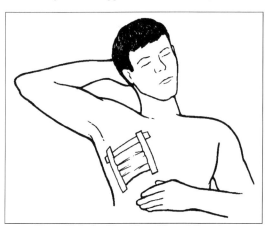

Figure V-5. Sucking Chest Wound Dressing

(b) Monitor the dressing and breathing.If breathing becomes more difficult, occasionally lift the untapped side of the dressing to allow trapped air to escape.

(4) Flail Chest:
  (a) Results from blunt trauma when three or more ribs are broken in two or more places. This section of broken ribs is referred to as a flail segment. When breathing in, the chest moves out while the flail segment moves in. When breathing out, the chest moves in while the flail segment moves out.
  (b) Immediately immobilize flail segment (place hand over area to prevent further motion).
  (c) Use tape (if available) to immobilize the flail segment.
  (d) Tape from breastbone to backbone on the injured side.
  (e) Do not surround the chest with tape.
  (f) If no tape, keep segment still with hand pressure or roll victim onto injured side to keep the segment still.
(5) Fractured ribs:
  (a) Encourage deep breathing (painful, but necessary to prevent the possible development of pneumonia).
  (b) Do not constrict breathing with tape.
d. Shock:
  (1) May be present with or without visible injury.
  (2) Treat the injury.
  (3) Maintain normal body temperature:
    (a) Remove wet clothing.
    (b) Give warm fluids.
    (c) Insulate from ground.
    (d) Shelter from the elements.
  (4) Elevate the legs six to eight inches unless there is a severe head or abdominal injury.
  (5) If very weak or unconscious:
    (a) Place victim on side to drain the mouth and prevent tongue from blocking airway.
    (b) Do not give oral fluids to an unconscious victim.
e. Treat fractures, sprains and dislocations:
  (1) Remove watches, jewelry, constricting clothing.
  (2) Dress wounds over fractures that penetrate the skin:
    (a) Clean wound if possible.
    (b) Apply dressings.
  (3) Place limb in as normal a position as possible.
  (4) Improvise splint with available materials:
    (a) Sticks; straight, stiff materials from equipment.
    (b) Secure to body parts; e.g., opposite leg or arm to chest.
  (5) Splint in position found if unable to move to a normal position.

NOTE: Fingers should be splinted in a slightly flexed position, NOT in straight position. Hand should look like it is grasping an apple.

---

  (6) For limb fractures, keep the fractured bones from moving by immobilizing the joints on both sides of the fracture.
  (7) For joint injuries, immobilize the bones on both sides of the joint.
  (8) Apply cold during first 24 hours after injury.

(9) Apply heat after the first 24 hours of injury.

(10) Use 15 to 20 minute periods of cold or heat application.

(11) Do not use continuous cold or heat therapy.

(12) Check periodically for a pulse beyond the injury.

2. **Common Injuries and Illnesses**
   a. Burns:
      (1) Cool as rapidly as possible in water.
      (2) Remove watches, jewelry, constricting clothing.
      (3) Do not remove embedded, charred material that will cause burned areas to bleed.
      (4) Cover with sterile dressings.
      (5) DO NOT use lotion or grease.
      (6) Avoid motion or rubbing of the burned part.
      (7) Drink water:
         (a) Burns increase fluid loss.
         (b) If possible, mix each quart with 1/4 teaspoon of salt.
      (8) Change dressings when soaked or dirty.
   b. Eye Injuries:
      (1) Sun/snow blindness (gritty, burning sensation and possible reduction in vision caused by sun exposure):
         (a) Close both eyes and cover lightly with light excluding dressings for 18 hours.
         (b) Wear eye protection or improvised sunglasses.
      (2) Foreign body in eye:
         (a) Irrigate with clean water from the inside to the outside corner of the eye.
         (b) If foreign body is not removed by irrigation, improvise a small swab. Moisten and wipe gently over the affected area.
         (c) If foreign body STILL not removed, patch eye for 24 hours, and then reattempt removal using steps (a) and (b) above.
   c. Heat Injury:
      (1) Heat Cramps (cramps in legs or abdomen):
         (a) Rest.
         (b) Drink water. If available, add 1/4 teaspoonful of salt per quart.
      (2) Heat exhaustion (pale; sweating; moist, cool skin):
         (a) Rest in shade.
         (b) Drink water.
         (c) Protect from further heat exposure.
      (3) Heat stroke (skin hot and flushed; sweating may or may not occur; fast pulse):

CAUTION: Handle heat stroke victim gently. Shock, seizures and cardiac arrest can occur.

         (a) Cool as rapidly as possible (saturate clothing with water and fan the victim).
         (b) Avoid overcooling.
         (c) Maintain airway, breathing and circulation.
   d. Cold injuries:
      (1) Frostnip and frostbite:
         (a) This is a progressive injury:

- Ears, nose, fingers and toes are affected first.
- Areas will feel cold and may tingle leading to . . .
- Numbness which progresses to...
- Waxy appearance with skin stiff and unable to glide freely over a joint.
(b) Frostnipped areas will rewarm with body heat.

> **NOTE:** Areas that cannot be rewarmed by body heat within 15 to 20 minutes of continuous skin to skin contact are classified as frostbite.

    (c) Frostbitten areas are deeply frozen and require medical treatment.
    (d) Do not rub frozen tissue.
    (e) Do not thaw frozen tissue.

> **CAUTION:** In frostbite, repeated freezing and thawing causes severe pain and increases damage to the tissue.

    (2) Hypothermia (lowering of body temperature to or below 95 degrees F or 35 degrees C):

> **CAUTION:** Handle hypothermia victim gently. Cardiac arrest can occur.

    (a) This is a progressive injury:
- Intense shivering with impaired ability to perform complex tasks goes to...
- Violent shivering, difficulty speaking, sluggish thinking goes to...
- Muscular rigidity with blue, puffy skin; jerky movements goes to...
- Coma, respiratory and cardiac failure.

    (b) Hypothermia treatment:
- Warm as rapidly as possible.
- Insulate against further heat loss; cover top of head.
- Pre-warm sleeping bag with two volunteers.
- Place casualty between two volunteers.
- Transfer body heat via skin to skin contact.
- Do not give fluids if consciousness is altered.

    (c) Put on dry clothing, if available.

e. Skin tissue damage:
    (1) Immersion injuries:
      (a) Skin becomes wrinkled as in "dishpan hands".
      (b) Avoid walking on affected feet.
      (c) Pat dry; don't rub. Skin tissue will be sensitive.
      (d) Dry socks and shoes. Keep feet protected.
      (e) Loosen boots, cuffs, etc. to improve circulation.
      (f) Do not apply creams or ointments.
      (g) Keep area dry, warm, and open to air.
    (2) Saltwater sores:
      (a) Change body positions frequently.
      (b) Keep sores dry.
      (c) Do not open or squeeze sores.

(d) Use antiseptic, if available.

f. Snakebites:

> **NOTE:** This snakebite treatment recommendation is for situations where medical aid and specialized equipment are not available.

    (1) Non-poisonous snakebite. Clean and bandage wound.

    (2) Poisonous snakebite:

        (a) Remove constricting items.

        (b) Minimize activity.

        (c) Do not cut the bite site; do not use your mouth to create suction.

        (d) Clean bite with soap and water, cover with a dressing.

        (e) Overwrap the bite site with a tight (elastic) bandage. (See Figure V-6). The intent is to slow capillary and venous blood flow, but not arterial flow. Check for pulse below the overwrap.

        (f) Splint bitten extremity to prevent motion.

        (g) Treat for shock.

        (h) Position extremity below level of heart.

        (i) If necessary construct shelter; let the victim rest.

        (j) For conscious victims, force fluids.

g. Marine life:

    (1) Stings:

        (a) Flush wound with salt water (fresh water stimulates toxin release).

        (b) Remove jewelry/watches.

        (c) Remove tentacles and gently scrape or shave skin.

        (d) Do not rub area with sand.

        (e) Apply a steroid cream, if available.

        (f) Treat for shock, artificial respiration may be required.

> **Note:** Do not use urine to flush or treat wounds.

    (2) Punctures:

        (a) Immerse affected part in hot water or apply hot compresses for 30-60 minutes (as hot as victim can tolerate).

        (b) Cover with clean dressing.

        (c) Treat for shock as needed.

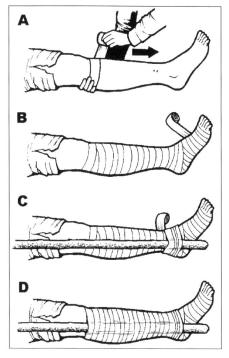

Figure V-6. Compression Bandage for Snake Bite

h. Skin irritants:
    (1) Include poison oak, poison ivy.
    (2) Wash with large amounts of water. Use soap, if available.
    (3) Keep covered to prevent scratching.
i. Infection:
    (1) Keep wound clean.
    (2) Use iodine tablet solution or diluted betadine to treat/prevent infection.
    (3) Change bandages as needed.
j. Cold, flu, etc, drink water, eat, rest, keep warm and dry.
k. Dysentery, diarrhea:
    (1) Drink water, liquid diet.
    (2) Consuming charcoal, made into paste may aid symptoms by absorbing toxins.
l. Constipation:
    (1) Normal.
    (2) Do not take laxatives.

      (3) Exercise.

      (4) Drink water.

m. Scurvy:

      (1) Lack of vitamin C.

      (2) Bleeding from gums, loosening of teeth, swelling in joints, wounds do not heal.

      (3) Eat raw greens, fruit.

      (4) Prepare evergreen tea:

         (a) Boil water.

         (b) While still very hot, immerse evergreen needles in water for 5 minutes.

         (c) Discard needles; drink liquid.

3. **Plant Medicine**

  a. Tannin:

      (1) Found in banana plants, common plantain, strawberry and blackberry stems and leaves, outer bark of all trees.

      (2) Preparation and use:

         (a) Place crushed outer bark, acorns, or dead leaves in water.

         (b) Leach out the tannin by soaking or boiling.

         (c) Replace depleted bark or plants with fresh material. Longer soaking or boiling increases the concentration of tannin.

         (d) Soak injured part.

         (e) Drink the cooled tea.

         (f) Apply as a compress by wetting a bandage

      (3) Burns:

         (a) Apply cooled tea compresses.

         (b) Pour cooled tea on burned area to ease pain.

         (c) Tea prevents infection and aids healing.

      (4) Skin problems (Dry rashes, fungal infections):

         (a) Cool compresses relieve itching.

         (b) Aids healing.

      (5) Lice:

         (a) Wash infested areas with warm or cooled tea.

         (b) Tea temporarily eases itching.

      (6) Diarrhea, dysentery and worms:

         (a) Drink strong tea solution.

         (b) Tea may promote voiding of worms.

  b. Willow and aspen (See Figure V-7):

      (1) Contain salicylic acid (component of aspirin).

      (2) Chew on twigs, buds, or cambium layer, the soft, moist layer between the outer bark and the wood.

      (3) Or, prepare tea as described under tannin. Drink the tea for colds and sore throat.

      (4) Reduces pain, inflammation, and fever.

      (5) For aches, pain and sprains, apply poultice:

         (a) Crush the plant or stems.

         (b) Make a pulpy mass.

(c) Hold in place over injury with a hot, moist dressing.

c. Cattail (See Figure V-7):
  (1) For wounds, sores, boils, inflammations, and burns.
  (2) Apply poultice of pounded roots.

d. Common Plantain (See Figure V-7):
  (1) Leaves contain many vitamins and minerals.
  (2) Relieves itching.
  (3) Use poultice of leaves for wounds, abrasions, stings.

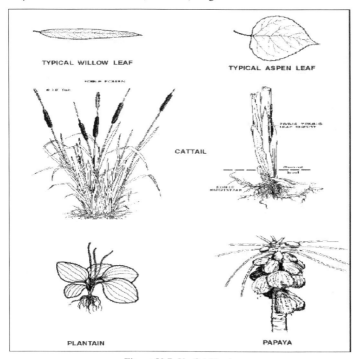

Figure V-7. Useful Plants

e. Papaya (See Figure V-7):
  (1) Milky white sap flowing from cuts in the unripe fruit contains Papuan which aids digestion; use as meat tenderizer.
  (2) Caution: The sap will cause a severe burning sensation if applied directly to wounds. Avoid getting sap into eyes.

4. **General Nutrition**
   a. Protein deficiency:
      (1) Irritability, loss of appetite, vomiting, diarrhea, muscular wasting, fluid retention.
      (2) Eat meat, fish, insects, and eggs.
      (3) Eat grains and nuts.
   b. Protein excess:
      (1) Can be fatal.
      (2) Occurs in long-term survival situations where only meat or fish is eaten.
      (3) Prevent by eating a varied diet with fruits and plants.
      (4) Eat the marrow from cooked bones for fat content.

5. **Sanitation and Hygiene**
   a. Stay clean:
      (1) Washing minimizes chance of infection.
      (2) Use white ashes, sand, or loamy soil as soap substitutes.
      (3) Exercise and short periods of exposure to sunshine and open air will help refresh the body.
   b. Lice, fleas, ticks, bedbugs, etc.:
      (1) Check body regularly.
      (2) Pick off and discard (including eggs). Do not crush.
      (3) Wash clothing and use repellents.
      (4) Use smoke to fumigate clothing and equipment.
   c. Hair:
      (1) Keep clean and combed.
      (2) Check for parasites.
   d. Mouth and teeth:
      (1) Brush daily.
      (2) Toothbrush use hardwood twig, fray it by chewing on one end then use as brush.
      (3) Single strand of an inner core string from parachute cord can be used for dental floss.
      (4) Gum tissues should be stimulated by rubbing with a clean finger.
      (5) Gargle with salt water to help prevent sore throats and aid in cleaning teeth/gums.
   e. Feet:
      (1) Change and wash socks daily.
      (2) Wash, dry, and massage feet daily.
      (3) Check feet frequently for blisters and red spots.
      (4) Use adhesive tape/mole skin to prevent further damage.

6. **Rules for Avoiding Illness**
   a. Disinfect all water obtained from natural sources.
   b. Use "cat hole" latrines 100 feet from natural water source.
   c. Wash hands before preparing food or water.
   d. Clean all eating utensils after each meal.
   e. Prevent insect bites by using repellent, netting and clothing.
   f. Dry wet clothing as soon as possible.
   g. Eat varied diet.
   h. Try to get 7-8 hours sleep per day.

Chapter XI

INDUCED CONDITIONS

NUCLEAR, BIOLOGICAL, AND CHEMICAL CONSIDERATIONS

1. **Nuclear**

> **Note:** Radiation protection depends on time of exposure, distance from the source, and shielding.

a. Protection:
   (1) **FIND PROTECTIVE SHELTER IMMEDIATELY**.
   (2) Time permitting, gather all equipment for survival.
   (3) Avoid detection and capture:
      (a) Seek existing shelter that may be improved (see Figure IX-1).

Figure IX-1. Immediate Action Shelter

   (b) If no shelter is available, dig a trench or foxhole:
      • Dig trench deep enough for protection, then enlarge for comfort (see Figure IX-2).
      • Cover with available material.

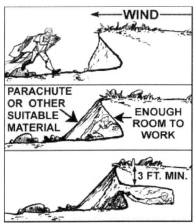

Figure IX-2. Improvised Shelter

(4) Radiation shielding effectiveness (see Figure IX-3).

NUCLEAR EXPLOSIONS: FALL FLAT. Cover exposed body parts. Present minimal profile to direction of blast. DO NOT LOOK AT FIREBALL. Remain prone until blast effects over.

SHELTER: Pick ASAP, 5 minutes unsheltered max. PRIORITY: (1) cave or tunnel covered with 3 or more feet of earth. (2) storm/storage cellars. (3) culverts. (4) basements. (5) abandoned stone/mud buildings. (6) foxhole 4 ft deep--remove topsoil within 2 ft radius of foxhole lip.

RADIATION SHIELDING EFFICIENCIES: One thickness reduces received radiation dose by one-half. Additional thickness added to any amount of thickness reduces received radiation dose by one-half.

Iron/Steel	.7 in	Earth	3.3 in	Wood (Soft)	8.8 in
Brick	2.0 in	Cinder Block	5.3 in	Snow	20.3 in
Concrete	2.2 in	Ice	6.8 in		

SHELTER SURVIVAL: KEEP CONTAMINATED MATERIALS OUT OF SHELTER. Good weather; bury contaminated clothing outside of shelter--recover later. Bad weather; shake strongly or beat with branches. Rinse and (or) shake wet clothing--DO NOT WRING OUT.

PERSONAL HYGIENE: Wash entire body with soap and ANY water; give close attention to fingernails and hairy parts. No water; Wipe all exposed skin surfaces with clean cloth or uncontaminated soil. Fallout/dusty conditions, keep entire body covered. Keep handkerchief/cloth over mouth and nose. Improvise goggles. DO NOT SMOKE.

No rate meter, complete isolation first 4-6 days after last explosion.

Day 3/7: Brief exposure, 30 minutes MAX.

Day 8: Brief exposure, 1 hour MAX.

Days 9-12: Exposure of 2-4 hours per day.

Day 13 on: Normal movement.

Figure IX-3. Radiation Shielding Efficiencies

(5) Leave contaminated equipment and clothing near shelter for retrieval after radioactive decay.

85

(6) Lie down, keep warm, sleep, and rest.
  b. Water/Food:
    (1) Water:
      (a) Allow no more than 30 minutes exposure on 3rd day for water procurement.
      (b) Water sources (in order of preference):
        • Springs, wells, or underground sources are safest.
        • Water in pipes / containers in abandoned buildings.
        • Snow, six or more inches below the surface during the fallout.
        • Streams and rivers (filtered before drinking).
        • Lakes, ponds, pools, etc.
        • Take water from below the surface, do not stir up the water.
        • Use a seep well.
      (c) Water preparation (see Figures IX-4 and IX-5):
        • Filtering through earth removes 99% of radioactivity.
        • Purify all water sources.

    (2) Food:
      (a) Processed foods (canned or packaged) are preferred, wash and wipe containers before use.
      (b) Animal foods:
        • Avoid animals that appear to be sick or dying.
        • Skin carefully to avoid contaminating the meat.
        • Before cooking, cut meat away from the bone, leaving at least 1/8 inch of meat on the bone.
        • Discard all internal organs.
        • Cook all meat until very well done.
      (c) Avoid:
        • Aquatic food sources; use only in extreme emergencies due to high concentration of radiation.
        • Shells of all eggs; contents will be safe to eat.
        • Milk from animals.
      (d) Plant foods (in order of preference):
        • Plants whose edible portions grow underground (for example, potatoes, turnips, carrots, etc.). Wash and remove skin.
        • Edible portions growing above ground which can be washed and peeled or skinned (bananas, apples, etc.).
        • Smooth skinned vegetables, fruits, or above ground plants, which are not easily peeled or washed.

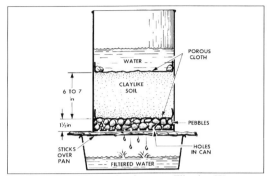

Figure IX-4. Filtration Systems, Filtering Water

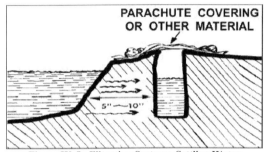

Figure IX-5. Filtration Systems, Settling Water

c. Self-aid:
  (1) General rules:
    (a) Prevent exposure to contaminants.
    (b) Use personal hygiene practices and remove body waste from shelter.
    (c) Rest; avoid fatigue.
    (d) Drink liquids.
  (2) Wounds:
    (a) Clean affected area.
    (b) Use antibacterial ointment or cleaning solution.
    (c) Cover with clean dressing.
    (d) Watch for signs of infection.
  (3) Burns:
    (a) Clean affected area.
    (b) Cover with clean dressing.
  (4) Radiation sickness (nausea, weakness, fatigue, vomiting, diarrhea, loss of hair, radiation burns):

87

        (a) Takes time to overcome.
        (b) Rest.
        (c) Drink fluids.
        (d) Maintain food intake.
        (e) Prevent additional exposure.

2. **Biological**
    a. Clues which may alert you to a biological attack:
        (1) Enemy aircraft dropping objects or spraying.
        (2) Breakable containers or unusual bombs, particularly those bursting with little or no blast, and muffled explosions.
        (3) Smoke or mist of unknown origin.
        (4) Unusual substances on the ground or vegetation; sick looking plants or crops.
    b. Protection from biological agents:
        (1) Use protective equipment.
        (2) Bathe as soon as the situation permits.
        (3) Wash hair and body thoroughly with soap and water.
        (4) Clean thoroughly under fingernails.
        (5) Clean teeth, gums, tongue, and roof of mouth frequently.
    c. Survival tips for biological conditions:
        (1) Keep your body and living area clean.
        (2) Stay alert for clues of biological attack.
        (3) Keep nose, mouth, and skin covered.
        (4) Keep food and water protected. Bottled or canned foods are safe if sealed. If in doubt, boil food and water for 10 minutes.
        (5) Construct shelter in a clear area, away from vegetation, with entrance 90 degrees to the prevailing wind.
        (6) If traveling, travel crosswind or upwind (taking advantage of terrain to stay away from depressions).

3. **Chemical**
    a. Detecting:
        (1) Smell—many agents have little or no odor.
        (2) Sight – many agents are colorless:
            (a) Color—yellow, orange, or red smoke or mist.
            (b) Liquid—oily, dark patches on leaves, ground, etc.
            (c) Gas—some agents appear as a mist immediately after shell burst.
            (d) Solid—most solid state agents have some color.
        (3) Sound—muffled explosions are possible indications of chemical agent bombs.
        (4) Feel—irritation to the nose, eyes, or skin and/or moisture on the skin are danger signs.
        (5) Taste—strange taste in food or water indicates contamination.
        (6) General indications—tears, difficult breathing, choking, itching, coughing, dizziness.
        (7) Wildlife—presence of sick or dying animals.
    b. Protection against chemical agents:

(1) Use protective equipment.
(2) Avoid contaminated areas:
    (a) Exit contaminated area by moving crosswind.
    (b) Select routes on high ground.
    (c) Avoid cellars, ditches, trenches, gullies, valleys, etc.
    (d) Avoid woods, tall grasses, and bushes as they tend to hold chemical agent vapors.
    (e) Decontaminate body and equipment as soon as possible:
        • Removing—pinch-blotting.
        • Neutralizing—warm water.
        • Destroying—burying.

c. Self aid in chemically contaminated areas:
(1) If a chemical defense ensemble is available:
    (a) Use all protective equipment.
    (b) Follow antidote directions when needed.
(2) If a chemical defense ensemble is not available:
    (a) Remove or tear away contaminated clothing.
    (b) Rinse contaminated areas with water.
    (c) Improvise a breathing filter using materials available (T-shirt, handkerchief, fabric, etc.).

d. Tips for the survivor:
(1) Do not use wood from a contaminated area for fire.
(2) Look for signs of chemical agents around water sources prior to procurement (oil spots, foreign odors, dead fish or animals).
(3) Keep food and water protected.
(4) Do not use plants for food or water in contaminated area.

THE WILL TO SURVIVE

ARTICLE VI CODE OF CONDUCT
I will never forget that I am an American fighting for freedom, responsible for my actions, and dedicated to the principles which made my country free. I will trust in my God and in the United States of America.

1. **Psychology of Survival**
   a. Be prepared:
      (1) Know your capabilities and limitations.
      (2) Keep a positive attitude. Lift yourself up.
      (3) Develop a realistic plan.
      (4) Anticipate fears.
      (5) Combating psychological stress:
          (a) Recognize and anticipate existing "stresses." (injury, death, fatigue, illness, hunger)
          (b) Attribute normal reactions to existing "stresses." (fear, anxiety, guilt, boredom, depression, anger)
          (c) Identify signals of distress created by "stresses." (indecision, withdrawal, forgetfulness, carelessness, and propensity to make mistakes)
   b. Strengthen your will to survive with:
      (1) The Code of Conduct.
      (2) Pledge of allegiance.
      (3) Faith in America.
      (4) Patriotic songs.
      (5) Thoughts of return to family and friends.
   c. Group Dynamics of survival:
      (1) Take care of your buddy.
      (2) Work as a team.
      (3) Reassure and encourage each other.
      (4) High morale is a result of group cohesiveness and well-planned organization:
          (a) Prevents panic.
          (b) Creates strength and trust in one another.
          (c) Favors persistency in overcoming failure.
          (d) Facilitates formulation of group goals to overcome obstacles.
      (5) Factors influencing group survival:
          (a) Enforce the chain of command.
          (b) Organize according to individual capabilities.
          (c) Accept suggestions and criticism.
          (d) Success often requires on-the-spot decision-making.
          (e) Confidence is gained through knowledge and survival skill proficiency.

PERSONAL SURVIVAL KITS

During the haste and confusion of combat, individuals may become separated from their issued survival kits. A personal survival kit should be carried for such a contingency. The limiting factors for such kits are bulk and weight. Three approaches to carrying personal survival kits should be considered: Scatter the items throughout clothing so the weight bulk is distributed over the body. This is also good insurance against loss of all of the kit, should a pocket not be fastened or ripped open. Pack items in one small container to make it easy to check for both location and contents.

The third method is a combination of the first two. By making several small kits (i.e. fishing, medical, and repair kits) and scattering these sub-kits throughout clothing to accomplish one task. This also decreases the chance of losing the smaller items. The packing of these items, regardless of which approach is used, is also important. The containers must small, sturdy, without sharp corners, and must provide protection for the kit contents. Some good containers are; plastic soap dishes, dental floss containers, film canisters, Band-Aid boxes, small leather or canvas patches, aspirin tins, heavy plastic bags, etc. If the container has a survival function such as a water container or signal mirror, so much the better. Small sharp items i.e., hooks, files, needles, razors and saw blades, are easily taped to a piece of thin cardboard and carried in a wallet.

The following is list of items to choose from when designing a personal survival kit for combat emergency needs:

Medical/Health Needs:

Sterile dressings	Personal medications
Small bar of odorless soap	Tweezers
Insect repellent	Betadine pads
Salt and sugar packets	Aspirin
Water purification tablets/straws	Mole skin
Chapstick/sunscreen	Handi-wipes
Assorted Band-Aids	Safety pins

Carrying/Holding Water:

Plastic bags	Surgical tubing
Plastic sheeting	Water tubing
Prophylactics	Ziplock bags
Heavy aluminum foil	

Body Protection:

Large plastic bag	Spare wool socks
Space blanket	Bandana/neckerchief
Evasion chart	Neck scarf/cravat
Floppy hat	Gloves
Wool watch cap	Sunglasses

PERSONAL SURVIVAL KITS

Camouflage Aid:

Camouflage sticks
Camouflage compact
Netting

Burlap
Socks (disguise boot prints)
Cammie scarf

Heat/Fires:

Matches (waterproof)
Cotton balls
Metal match
Magnesium block

Small candle
Lighter
Magnifying glass
Petroleum gauze pads

Repairing/Improvising:

Multi-bladed pocket knife
Single edge razor blades
Small sharpening stone
Flexible wire saw
Duct/electrical tape

Para 550 cord
Assorted needles
Safety pins
Safety wire
Heavy thread

Navigation/Travel:

Evasion chart
Area topographic map
Compass
Small pencil
Small high quality monocular

Signal mirror
Spare radio battery
Pen light
Whistle

Food Procurement:

Fish hooks (assorted)
Sinkers
Bouillon cubes

Nets
Lures/spinners/flies
Snare wire

RECOMMENDED READING LIST

FIVE YEARS TO FREEDOM
Maj. James N. Rowe

SEVEN YEARS IN HANOI
Capt. Larry Chesley

**IN THE PRESENCE OF THINE
ENEMIES**
Capt. Howard Rutledge

THE PASSING OF THE NIGHT
Col. Robinson Risner

THEY WOULDN'T LET US DIE
Stephen A. Rowan

I'M NO HERO
Joseph C. Plum

SEVEN YEARS IN HELL
LtCol. Jay R. Jensen

PRISONER
Maj. Theodore Gostas

**SEARCH AND RESCUE IN
SOUTHEAST ASIA, 1961-1975**
Office of USAF History,
Washington D.C.

THE GREAT ESACPE
Paul Brickhill

MISSING IN ACTION
James C. Roberts

BEFORE HONOR
Eugene B. McDaniel

**PRISONER OF WAR: SIX YEARS
IN HANOI**
M. McGrath

P.O.W.
John H. Hubble

**P.O.W.: TWO YEARS WITH THE
VIET CONG**
George E. Smith

AN AMERICAN IN THE GULAG
Alexander Dulgun & Patrick
Watson

PASSWORD IN COURAGE
John Castle

MARCH TO CALUMNY
A. Biderman

**THIS WAS ANDERSONVILLE: THE
TRUE STORY OF ANDERSONVILLE
MILITARY PRISON**
John McElroy

SECOND IN COMMAND
E.R. Murphy

**A PRISONER'S DUTY: GREAT
ESCAPES IN U.S. MILITARY
HISTORY**
R.C. Doyle

HANOI COMMITMENT
James A. Mulligan

**THE ENDLESS HOURS: 2 1/2
YEARS AS A PRISONER OF THE
CHINESE COMMUNISTS**
Wallace L. Brown

**UNITED STATES MARINES IN
NORTH CHINA**
John A. White

CAPTURED
Carolyn P. Miller

PRISONERS OF WAR
A.J. Barker

BUCHER, MY STORY
CDR Lloyd M. Bucher

OPERATION OVERFLIGHT: THE
U-2 SPY PILOT TELLS HIS
STORY
Francis G. Powers & C.
Gentry

CHAINED EAGLE
Everette Alvarez & Anthony
S. Pitch

A CODE TO KEEP
Ernest Brace

THE INTERROGATOR: THE STORY
OF HANNS JOACHIM SCHARFF,
MASTER INTERROGATOR OF THE
LUFTWAFFE
R.F. Toliver

HONOR BOUND: THE HISTORY OF
AMERICAN PRISONERS OF WAR
IN SOUTHEAST ASIA, 1961-
1973
Stuart I. Rochester &
Frederick T. Kiley

ESCAPE FROM LAOS
Dieter Dengler

SOME SURVIVED
Manny Lawton

TORNADO DOWN
John Peters & John Nichol

THE ONE THAT GOT AWAY
Chris Ryan

FM 21-76: SURVIVAL

AFM 64-4: SURVIVAL TRAINING

OUTDOOR SURVIVAL SKILLS
Larry Dean Olsen

SURVIVAL AFLOAT
Don Biggs

SAS SURVIVAL HANDBOOK
L. Wiseman

CAMPING AND WILDERNESS
SURVIVAL
P. Trawell

JAMES B. STOCKDALE READING
LIST:

THOUGHTS OF A PHILOSOPHICAL
FIGHTER PILOT

TEN YEARS OF REFLECTION, A
VIETNAM EXPERIENCE

ETHICS OF CITIZENSHIP, 1981

IN LOVE AND WAR

COURAGE UNDER FIRE

FOUNDATIONS OF MORAL
OBLIGATION, THE STOCKDALE
COURSE
J.R. Brennan

HERBAL MEDICINE
D. D. Buchman

Made in the USA
Middletown, DE
01 December 2018